Mike's Underpants and Other Tales of Travel

Allan Bate

Text copyright© 2017
Allan Bate

All Rights Reserved

For my wife Ann, sons Steven and Stuart, their wives Natascha and Anne Marie, grandchildren Sarah, Michael, Sebastien, Daniel, Andrew and my brothers and sister. Also a special mention for Mike and Margaret, Lewis and Jan, Joe and Sylvia and Colin and Jean who have shared some of our travel experiences.

Table of Contents

Foreword.. 6
1. Early Travels and the Welsh Riviera..... 7
2. From Grasmere to the World............... 58
3. Mike's Underpants............................... 79
4. Kettles, Keys, Kerfuffle, Kerkyra and Kamikaze…….97
5. Petra, Sinai and The Coloured Canyon….. 129
6. Bats, Fireflies and Other Natural Phenomena…158
7. Unusual Occurrences......................... 176
8. Sake, Sashimi, Noodles, Vodka Andouillette and other Delicacies...216
9. When Irish Eyes are Smiling.............. 246
10. Animal Antics................................... 265
11. Human Antics................................... 281
12. Sunsets... 300
Epilogue.. 320

Foreword

Have you ever had a lovely, relaxing holiday in an idyllic setting? The weather is perfect, everything goes to plan, and the food is great ...

But sometimes things don't always go so smoothly. Sometimes things go wrong. Sometimes the unexpected happens...

Those holidays and travels which are most memorable are often the ones when things go wrong or when you have a chance meeting or an unexpected experience or a comical situation.

This travel log is about those minor inconveniences and surprising occurrences. Of course, holidays affected by great tragedy such as the Tsunami which swept across the south east coastlands of Asia are remembered in the global conscience with much sadness and sympathy for those who suffered.

1. Early Travels and the Welsh Riviera

As a child I always had a great interest in Geography and a strong desire to travel to faraway and exotic places. My favourite books as a ten year old were The Coral Island, Treasure Island, Robinson Crusoe, The Swiss Family Robinson, Gulliver's Travels and, a bit later on, when I was at Grammar School –"The Lord of The Flies".

My passion for Geography, maps, and all places foreign was shared, somewhat forcibly, by some of my siblings. I say some because we were, at the final count, a family with seven children. My eldest brother (Bert) and sister (Rita) were already nearly grown up at this time and were more interested in motorbikes, girls, pop stars, boys, make- up, weight training, shopping and all those pursuits of older teenagers.

So, at the age of nine and ten, I had a class of two in our kitchen classroom. My youngest brother (Geoff) was still a toddler and therefore not a viable member of our "school". My youngest sister (Gillian) was yet to be born. One of my "pupil brothers" was a year older than me (Dennis) and the other a year younger (Rodney). When we played at making films such as Moby Dick, Apache River, Tarzan, Flash Gordon - Hero of The Universe in our kitchen set we were, all three of us, actors, directors, producers and props experts. Water from the sink, splashed all over your face and hair, made the harpooning of Moby Dick in a small rowing boat all the more realistic. Chairs tied together and placed next to the old kitchen range made a fantastic covered wagon or stagecoach. Sitting on the metal hotplates of the kitchen range with your feet on the chairs which had ropes from the shed tied to them made great reins to urge your horses on faster as Apache arrows whistled over your head. And who could resist the yodelling call of Tarzan as you jumped on your vine and swung from the kitchen range tree onto a rogue lion (usually your younger brother) to wrestle with it and finally kill it. In all these productions we shared the directions and story lines but my older brother had to be the star, the hero. Being older was nearly always the criterion in these matters. I say, nearly always, because when it came to the "kitchen school" I was always the teacher and they were always the pupils.

On the old kitchen range I would prop up a small blackboard. I would draw maps of Britain, Africa,

South America and the other continents and mark on them the main mountains, rivers, lakes and cities. My brothers would copy them onto the back of old wallpaper cut into page sized strips. Then they had to memorise them ready for the oral and written tests I gave them at the end of the week. But I also gave them bits of fascinating (to me at least) information which I'd gleaned from school, books, atlases. I told them about the highest waterfall in the world, the Angel Falls in Venezuela, South America, which had the highest single drop of about 2,600 feet. I told them how an American aviator, Jimmie Angel, flew over the falls and tried to land on top. When the wheels of the aeroplane got stuck in the marshy ground, he, his wife and two companions had to descend on foot taking them eleven days. I told them about the Great Pyramid in Egypt on the River Nile, the longest river in the world. I told them about the Red Rose City of Petra which had been carved from the rocks. I told them about the Himalayas and Mount Everest, the highest mountain in the world. I told them about the Great Wall of China and Death Valley in the USA and the volcanoes such as Vesuvius and Etna. I told them about the great eruption of Krakatoa, east of Java in the Indian Ocean , which sent a tidal wave over one hundred feet high to the coasts, killing over 30,000 people; and how the explosion could be heard three thousand miles away in Africa. And so I would go on, thinking that both my brothers would be just as interested as I was in these fascinating places.

This, however, was the extent of my travel experiences at that time - theory and books and imagination! Theory, books and imagination were always perfect. No problems tainted your vision, your expectations. But even from my first experiences of travel things were not always so perfect. If things could go wrong they would.

In reality the furthest I'd been was a day trip to Southport - eighteen miles away! To me, at the age of ten, it was like travelling beyond the Pillars of Hercules, as the double decked bus squeezed its way through the Jaws of Ormskirk and on to unknown territories of the South - East Lancashire plain. Arriving at the bus station we walked down Lord Street then turned up left towards the Promenade and the amusement arcades. A few pennies in the slot machines and an ice cream were the extent of our extravagance. A boat on the Marina, a trip on the miniature railway, a visit to the fairground, a round of crazy golf, a tour of the little zoo were expenditures out of our reach. A walk along the pier and back was a welcome distraction culminating in the main item on the agenda - the sands of Southport beach. Exploring Southport Sands in a vain attempt to find the sea, paddling in pools left by some prehistoric tide, playing football and cricket, eating gritty sandwiches washed down by a bottle of diluted orange were the main activities of our excursion.

However, at that time, places visited on "family travels" (not actually to be found in "Unforgettable Places to see before you die") and ticked off the list, actually numbered three. Second on the list was a trek to Billinge Hill (some five miles away), having travelled along the banks of the Sankey Brook, the Blackbrook Canal and crossing the mighty A580 (East Lancashire Road - from Liverpool to Manchester) was always a favourite. Our third, far flung destination was "Happy Valley" (No, not Hong Kong!) which lay between Carr Mill Dam (famed in those days for holding the World Power Boat Championships) and Carr Mill Wood. Here, on a hot Sunday afternoon, we would lounge on the grassy slopes and paddle in the open bricked culvert which was an overflow from the Dam into Black Brook itself.

Even then, though, we had "Gap Days", when my brothers and I would travel independently to see the world. The "Hotties" was one such Mecca. The "Hotties" was our Caribbean beach or our warm lagoon on the Great Barrier Reef. It was in fact the Sankey Canal excavated by the Sankey Navigation Company. It was used to transport raw materials such as coal, Shirdley Hill sand, potash and other chemicals to a booming chemical industry in St.

Helens, especially to the glass making factories of Pilkington Brothers which was sited along its banks. Glass making was a continuous process and hot water used in the glass cooling process was piped into the canal. So the waters of the canal were permanently warm. It was like some hot spring spa bath in Rotorua, New Zealand or in Iceland. We swam there on many an occasion, diving under the murky brown water in the hope of glimpsing the tropical fish which darted in and out of the wrecks which lay on the bottom - bicycles and prams that is! Some pet shop owner had once tipped their aquariums of tropical fish into the "Hotties" and it was rumoured that they survived and bred in the hot waters. But we never sent postcards to our parents or went back with tales of our adventures because at least one person per year had drowned in the "Hotties".

Another hazardous environment which we tackled, and looking back was our Inca Trail, was the Indian Trail. But this wasn't in the far flung Andes of Peru. It was in The Chemics. It didn't lead to Machu Picchu but it lead to the Big Cave. The Chemics (local dialect - Kimmicks) were extensive spoil heaps of cinder and baked chemicals left behind as a monument to the chemical industry which had once flourished close to our house. A huge explosion at the Kurtz Chemical Works in 1899 was probably the last straw and the industry moved elsewhere except for glass making for which there was great demand.

My one-year older brother was always the leader of expeditions. He liked to think he was Scott of the Antarctic, Stanley and Livingstone and Thor Heyerdahl, all rolled into one. So he was in charge and he made us walk the Indian Trail. This was a narrow path which wound round the side of a chemical heap cliff (known to us as Big Kimmick) which had a precipitous drop to the Sankey Brook below. He, the mountain goat, would trip deftly to the Big Cave, and watching us struggle inch by inch along the trail, would gently encourage us by making powder bombs from the clay-like chemical waste and throwing them so that they exploded on the narrow path just in front of our feet. We shouted and swore but it achieved its desired effect and we almost ran the rest of the way to reach the sanctuary of the Big Cave. By the time we had reached this goal our jumpers and trousers were covered in yellow and white dust. And really the most hazardous part of the whole expedition was dusting yourself down afterwards and getting into the bathroom for wet sponging before the eagle eyes of our mother spotted us.

Snow sports were another of our passions. But we didn't travel to the Alps or even Aviemore. Our ski slopes were in - you've guessed it - The Chemics. During one particularly harsh winter we had greater snowfalls than usual and deep drifts of snow covered the slopes of The Chemics. The Big Chemics dropped down to a cinder plateau ridge called the Little Chemics which ended in a rounded spur (not truncated by Ice Age glaciers but dumped by trucks and plied up by cranes) known to us as Big Hill. The snow slopes of Big Hill were too tempting. So in that particular year (with snow quality to match the best slopes of Europe) one year older brother, Nanook of The North, led an expedition to the off piste runs of Big Hill. Accompanying him and wrapped in scarves and wearing balaclavas (compulsory headgear in those days), duffle coats and wellingtons, were one year younger brother, Gilly Marsh and me. Trudging through the snowdrifts of The Fields, the great grassy wasteland which led to The Chemics, we carried pieces of flattened cardboard boxes. For us there were no such things as wooden sleds with smooth metal runners or plastic sledges. But when you've got an inspirational leader like one year older brother then survival in the wilderness by (as he used to say) "thinking out of the square" meant you could achieve anything. And so it was that he discovered a large piece of corrugated tin lying discarded amongst frozen grass in a snow filled hollow. It had been part of the school's football field fence which adjoined The Fields.

My younger brother and I stood on the corrugated sheet whilst older brother and Gilly Marsh pulled and pushed and bent over the end to make a super, streamlined, four man toboggan. Fifteen minutes later we had hauled and dragged it to the summit of Big Hill. The snow covered slopes swept down to a narrow path which ran all along that edge of the Little Chemics separating them from the steep embankment which fell to the Sankey Brook below. Here its dark crimson colour stood out against the white slopes of the embankment. The day before it had been a lurid pea green colour. Each day it changed to match the chemicals pumped in further upstream by the Plastics and Cellophane plant. We gazed upon a truly stupendous Cresta Run.

With assurances from one year older brother that this would be an exciting but safe toboggan run, (he claimed the path would slow down our descent and the low levee which edged the Brook at this point would bring us to a stop) my younger brother and I knelt on the back and older brother and Gilly Marsh standing at either side of the bent over front began to run and push. As the front end tipped over the edge of the slope they both jumped on clinging tightly onto the front end. We gathered speed rapidly. There was no way of controlling the missile. It rushed down the slope at a colossal speed. Then, as predicted by older brother, we hit the path. Instead of slowing us down the toboggan leapt through the air like a ski jumper and, as it crashed down onto the snow slopes of the embankment, my younger brother and I toppled off into a deep patch of snow. Gilly Marsh clung on but was tipped off sideways as the toboggan rushed headlong towards the Sankey Brook. My one year older brother was wrong about the path slowing us down but he was certainly right about the levee. The toboggan came to a sudden halt as the front end drove in the snow drift which was plastered against the levee. Still clinging onto the front end my brother was catapulted forward looking like a spread - eagled flying squirrel and landed in the icy, crimson coloured waters of the Sankey Brook. This time, when we went home, none of us avoided the final hazard of our expedition.

Some travels go smoothly and are uneventful; others sometimes go wrong and are memorable. Another such expedition in those early days was a trip to Carr Mill Wood. My one year older brother was going on a trek with his best friend, Gilly Marsh. He was the same age as my brother but a lot bigger and stronger. Was it because he was an only child? I don't know but on that day I was desperate to go with them. However, my brother was not so keen on the idea and politely told me to "bugger off". I said I'd go and tell my mum that he was swearing if he didn't let me go with them. He just said, 'Go on then.' I knew and he knew that if I carried out this threat they would be free of me and would be quickly on their way. This only increased my desire and so I followed them at what I thought was a safe distance. My brother tried gentle persuasion by throwing stones at me every time I popped up from behind a mound or out of a group of trees. In the end he gave up and so I tagged along. When we got to the wood we spent some time trying to dam the stream which ran through it with stones and rocks and sods. Then we had fencing tournaments with Rose Bay Willow Herb stalks. You stripped off all the leaves and the purple flower heads and they made perfect foils. When we were tired of that we decided on Olympic Javelin throwing. Gilly Marsh won easily because he was so tall and big and strong. But, in the end, we turned to the only true "adventure holiday" activity in a wood - climbing trees. And that's when things went wrong!

Along the path, bowing over the parapet of a small footbridge, was a very tempting tree. Its lowest branches were only about seven or eight feet from the ground and it was so gnarled that it was rich in hand and foot holds. Gilly Marsh had romped away through the ferns deeper into the wood but my brother and I both climbed easily into the fork of the tree. My brother moved out along the branch, holding onto the trunk. He was shouting to Gilly Marsh when he became unbalanced. He swayed backwards, his hands left the trunk and he tottered and teetered for long seconds. But he was unable to regain his balance. Falling backwards, he whirled his arms trying to grasp thin air and managed to drop onto his feet but he landed more heavily on his left foot and toppled over. I was just laughing at the sight when I realised he was moaning and groaning and wasn't getting to his feet. I clambered down and my brother was obviously in real pain. Shouting for Gilly Marsh, I tried to get him to his feet but he swore at me, now in real pain. Between us, Gilly and I lifted him with one arm round each of our shoulders. My brother was now crying with the pain. Knowing that he needed some medical attention we immediately tried to make a move down the path. He was hopping on his right foot which was undamaged, supported by the two of us. Because I was a lot shorter than Gilly Marsh, movement was awkward and progress was very slow.

We stopped. We knew it would be too difficult to get him home in this way. In the end Gilly Marsh gave my brother a piggy back all the way home - non-stop - a distance of three miles! My brother had broken nearly every bone in his left ankle and spent six weeks in hospital.

It is certainly those travels which go wrong in some way which are memorable.

- - -oOo- - -

My first real holiday, though, came when I was eleven years old, in the summer holidays before I started at the local grammar school. The whole family went to Towyn, near Rhyl, in Wales. This was a genuine holiday - our very first! After all it was to a foreign country. A week at the seaside was the envy of our friends. So one Saturday, in August, we excitedly loaded our luggage into the back of an old white minibus. It belonged to one of my father's workmates and, for the price of the fuel, he agreed to take us to Towyn and pick us up the following Saturday. Two old brown suitcases, one grey suitcase with red speckles and an old canvas holdall (each one bound with a brown leather belt) were loaded into the back. My father sat up front with my eldest brother and the driver. Mum, sister, and the four boys were all squeezed into the back. There were no motorways in those days so we drove down to the Widnes - Runcorn Bridge, crossed the Mersey and the Manchester Ship Canal and continued on to Frodsham.

We played games like counting a chosen colour of motor car and seeing who could spot the most. By the time we had reached Frodsham we were arguing and repeatedly asking the age old question "Are we there yet?" The sights of first, Beacon Hill overlooking Frodsham and then, further on, the crags of Helsby Hill held our attention for a while. I remember remarking to my two geography pupils that these escarpments would probably have once been a cliff line and the flat Cheshire Plain we were travelling along would have been the sea. Whether or not it was because we were not in the 'kitchen classroom', they chose to ignore me and carried on arguing with each other. Then we all started arguing and wrestling with each other. My mum diverted our attention by devising a competition for the first person to spot a cow.

Motoring onwards we by passed Queensferry and went past RAF Sealand. We spotted the World War II fighter plane on display in front of the main building. My father said it was a Spitfire and we could see the blue outer circle with a red centre painted on the side and looking like a target. This was a short diversion from the pained cries of "Are we there yet?" which had arisen again. Immediately my mother quelled the moaning and arguing with another of her competitions. 'First one to spot the sea gets a threepenny bit,' she said. 'It'll probably be on your right.' We all jostled and shuffled across the seats and craned our necks to peer out of the windows on the right hand side.

Following the signs to Flint and Holywell, we headed towards the coast or, more accurately, the estuary of the River Dee. When my one year older brother shouted excitedly, 'There it is! The sea!' we all groaned, 'It's not fair!' and

'Couldn't see because of his big head!'

'Don't worry, there'll be another chance when we get near to Rhyl. There'll be a sixpence for the first one to spot the proper sea.'

Then we turned off and headed cross country towards Trelawnyd and Dyserth. The driver, my dad's friend, shouted back to us that there was a waterfall at Dyserth and we could stop there for a break. But he had to stop sooner because my one year younger brother felt sick. He was duly sick in a hedgerow at the side of the road.

After a brief viewing of Dyserth Falls we moved on towards Rhyl. Passing through Rhuddlan, we continued down the A525 skirting Rhyl and driving down the coast road. We had all spotted the sea at the same time and were promised threepence each to spend at the Amusement Arcade. Crossing the River

Clwyd, we passed through Kimnel Bay arriving, at last, along the busy main road, at the small resort of Towyn.

We turned right down Sandy Lane and were told by the driver that our holiday camp, Edwards' Camp, was at the end of this road and quite close to the sea wall and beach. With great excitement, pointing and shouting, we spotted the Amusement Arcade. People thronged into the Arcade. There were bright, flashing lights and the pinging and buzzing of all the slot machines. The driver signalled to turn left as he pointed through his windscreen, proclaiming, 'Straight ahead! Look! The railway track and just beyond that the sea wall.'

We could see, in the distance, a stepped concrete wall. Steps went up to a walkway. People were walking along the top; some had stopped and were leaning on the upper wall to look out to the sea; others were climbing up steps over the wall to get onto the beach.

In a short distance we passed through a large gateway. Arched above this was a sign which said, "Welcome to Edwards' Holiday Camp." We had arrived. My first proper holiday. My first visit to a foreign country.

The minibus pulled up outside two low buildings. One was a shop. The other was like an office. My father jumped out, clutching a piece of paper, and strode into the office. Five minutes later he reappeared, waving a set of keys in his hand. Keys to our holiday chalet.

'Helensolme!' my father exclaimed proudly, pointing to the nameplate attached to the key ring. 'Ours for the week!'

Chalet! Ever since my parents had mentioned going to a holiday chalet in Towyn, I'd formed a picture in my mind. I'd seen drawings and photographs of Swiss chalets in books at school. Ornate carvings around the roof and eaves, pretty shutters on the windows, window boxes of multi – coloured flowers, brightly painted steps, a beautiful meadow full of wild flowers, all came flooding back into my mind.

As the tarmacked drive petered out we bounced and swayed along a rough track full of potholes and toothed with hard, sharp flints sticking up above the surface. On either side we passed rows of caravans interspersed with shacks. I thought these probably housed tools and lawn mowers. How wrong I was!

'Which field? We've just passed Fields A and B,' said our driver.

'We're on G,' replied my father.

Then the minibus slowed at crossroads. To the right a post, leaning precariously, had a wooden arrow nailed to the top of it. To the left was a similar signpost. On the left hand post it said, "C, D, E" and on the right was painted, "F, G, and H". We turned right towards G field. A square plaque on a low post showed a large letter F painted roughly in black. We drove through F field which was row upon row of caravans.

G field must be for all the chalets, I thought. It was. But not the chalets of my imagination. We pulled up to the letter G signpost and then dropped left from the path and drove along the grass. Here was a more open field with two lines of low wooden bungalows or shacks down either side and about three caravans down the middle. We stopped outside a low, wooden shack.

'Here we are,' shouted my father. 'Helensolme!'

My mouth dropped open. I just stared and stared out of the window. I wanted to shout out, 'No! There must be some mistake. This isn't a chalet. It's a shack, just a shack!'

I was bundled out of the door by my two brothers and I just stood and stared. My brothers were helping to unload the minibus but all I could do was stare. It was like a shack out of one of those Hill Billy films – Ma and Pa Kettle – but not as big. It was just squatting there amongst the long tussocks of grass. The roof was low and covered in green roofing felt. Set into the roof were four squares of glass which acted as skylights. A narrow strip of grass, the front garden of the shack, was bounded by a wire fence. Two wires formed the fence which ran all the way round the perimeter of Helensolme. In front of the door they were attached to two wooden posts which were splayed apart and looked as though they would collapse the first time anyone leant on them. Once through this "gateway" a single wooden step led up to the narrow front door which was painted dark green. The door surround was built out of strips of wood which looked like pieces of floorboard. Above the door was a small wooden, triangular canopy. It looked like someone's amateurish attempt at creating the effect of the entrance to an Egyptian Pyramid.

To the left of the doorway was a bay window. The wooden window frame was painted roughly in thick white gloss. One of the panes had been cracked or broken and had been mended with tape and putty. The white curtains, patterned with green and red flowers, were drawn to. This was one bedroom. To the right of the door was a larger bay window. The woodwork was painted in the same white. On the white, attached sill just below the window, in black metal capital letters, was the name - "HELENSOLME". An even larger crack in one pane was repaired with the thick white putty and tape. Further to the right was a matching bay window to the left one. It had the same patterned curtains. This was the other bedroom. The wooden walls of "Helensolme" were painted in dark green to match the door. "Helensolme" did not exactly proclaim comfort or the promise of a relaxing holiday. To me it was more a hurdle to be overcome.

Each one of us carried a bag or a case and squeezed into the main and only living space. There was a fusty smell which pervaded every corner of the gloomy room. The flooring, covered in a yellow lino with a black and red square pattern, rose in the middle of the room and sloped noticeably down at either side to the bedrooms. It was as if there was some huge giant lying below trying to force his way out, I thought at the time. A runner of carpet, patterned heavily with leaves and rusty flowers, stretched across the middle of the room ending at each bedroom door. On the wall opposite the door was a brownstone sink, a wooden draining board and a Formica work top. There were cupboards below and, half way along, a cream coloured oven with gas rings surrounded by patches of brown grease. There was a small window above the sink and a long wall cupboard. Crouched at either side of the room were two red velvety armchairs with wooden arms. It had seen better days. Rips in the material had been repaired with tape. Under the large bay window was a large, square rug. It was red and threadbare along the edges. On top of this was a drop – leaved table with several chairs, some wooden, some painted white. The table was draped with a tartan tablecloth. On each wall was a gas mantle covered with a yellow glass globe. This was our exotic chalet!

Mother had done a quick survey of the premises and we were assigned to bedrooms. The boys were to occupy the left side bedroom and mother, father and sister the one to the right. Bundling our bags into the bedroom, we marked out our territory. There were two double beds which sagged in the middle. Squeezed between them was a small wooden stool, painted green, with a paraffin lamp on it. On the wall next to the door was a set of drawers with a mirror above and another paraffin lamp standing on a doily. This wasn't a place for creature comforts so, after a few seconds, three other brothers and myself, had run outside to explore the domain.

We ran around the perimeter of our holiday home and discovered that, at the back, was a ditch which smelt thickly of stagnant water. Then younger brother said, 'What's those two metal things with the tubes?'

Gathering round, we examined them. Older brother declared confidently, 'They are the Calor Gas canisters to send the gas for the gas lights and cooker.'

Our excitement at finding a colony of toads hopping and jumping through the long grass was halted by our eldest brother.

'Hey, you lot! Come on! I've got to take you to the Arcade unless you want to stay here.'

As one we charged at eldest brother, shouting and laughing. Whilst my parents and older sister were unpacking and getting things "shipshape", my eldest brother had been assigned to taking us to the Amusement Arcade. We'd each been given sixpence.

Sixpences were changed into pennies. I lost my first penny on The Penny Falls Machine. It looked so easy just to drop a penny onto the edge of the Falls so that it would push against a pile of pennies hanging over the edge and send them cascading out of the machine and into my waiting hands. Instead the penny slipped and overlapped its neighbours forming an even more tantalizing pile teetering on the very edge of the Falls. But I won three pennies on the Silver Cup Machine. Flicking the lever, I sent the ball bearing whizzing round the circular metal track until it dropped down into the Win Cup. Like everyone else, though, with extra pennies to spend, I was happy to carry on. I lost the three pennies on the Crane Grab trying to pick up a red toy car which I probably didn't really want anyway. It wasn't long before we'd all spent up and made our way back to Helensolme.

My father had been to the fish and chip shop and we all had tea sitting round the big table by the bay window. After tea we were allowed to play outside on the grassy meadow. We played hide and seek and football and we looked for toads and frogs along the edge of the ditch. And we played "piggy". One year older brother sharpened each end of a small piece of wood with his penknife. We all hunted for a longer twig or piece of wood which would be the striker. The "piggy" was placed on the ground. Hitting a pointed end with the striker made the "piggy" jump into the air. Then you had to whack it with the striker to hit it as far away as possible. You challenged the next person to reach where the "piggy" had landed in a specified number of strides. If they didn't succeed you were awarded that number of points and got another go at striking the "piggy". If they did reach it in that number of strides they got the points and became the striker. This was all part of our holiday entertainment. No need for Butlin's Redcoats!

However the sky suddenly darkened. Very soon there was a fork of lightning and a crack of thunder. Rain suddenly fell very heavily. From the door my father ordered us all inside. But the holiday entertainment didn't end there.

Gas mantles were lit. We all sat round the table with the frowzy smell of calor gas and the fitful glow from the wall lights. A bag of halfpennies was divided between us and we played gin rummy. The winner took the "pot" of halfpennies which each one of us had thrown into the centre of the table. The third game was interrupted when eldest brother jumped up, wiping his neck and exclaiming, 'Something's dripping on my neck!'

The rain was battering on the roof and against the window panes. And sure enough we spotted a steady drip of water falling from the ceiling on to eldest brother's head. Someone else spotted a drip splashing onto the kitchen work top. Then it was "hunt the drips". There were some in both bedrooms. Pans, plastic jugs and other containers were placed judiciously below each leak. When every leak had been dealt with we returned to our game of cards. There was something pleasurable and satisfying about being altogether, around the table, in the dim flickering gaslight, with the drip – dripping of leaks and the steady rhythm of the rain against the window pane.

Gin rummy ran its course and the last game finished. It was then that a plaintive voice from youngest brother piped up:

'Tell us a story, dad. A ghost story!'

'Yeh, yeh! A ghost story! A ghost story! Please…'

Mum shot a withering glance at dad to register her disapproval but whether he saw it or ignored it I don't know.

'All right, all right! Sit you down on the floor and get comfy.'

Then dad launched into one of his famous stories.

'It was one night in summer. We'd gone to bed and I was fast asleep. It must have been about two o'clock in the morning when your mother nudges me and says, "Are you awake …"

'An' you weren't because, as usual, you were snoring loud enough to wake the dead…'

'Well, yes, I was fast asleep. Until, of course, this sharp pain in my ribs and this talking in my ear wakes me up. Being half asleep I says what's the matter? Can't you hear it? says your mother. Hear what? I says. That, says your mother. I can't hear anything, I says. If you'll shut up an' listen – shhhh, says your mother. So I goes quiet and listens. But there's not a sound. I was just going to say, it's O.K. go back to sleep when I heard this clanking noise. There! What's that then? says your mother. It's burglars, she says, that's what! So I listens again. And I could hear it again. It was a clinking and a clanking. Down the side of the house. It was like a chain being dragged along the ground. Well I was scared I can tell you. Well, what are you gonna do? says your mother. Go and see who it is before we're all murdered in our beds. So I gets out of bed and creeps down stairs. I stops halfway and listens. But the dragging and clanking are getting louder, nearer and nearer to the porch at the back door. I carries on down and then I grabs a poker from the hearth. I creeps up to the back door, stands still and listens. Not a noise. Clanking stopped. Quietly, I turns the key in the lock of the back door. Is it a ghost dragging its chains? I thinks. Raising the poker I turns the knob and opens the door fast. And there in front of me is a horse's head. A great bloomin' white horse, its head and front legs in our back porch. Round its neck is a long chain and tied to the end of it a metal stake. It snorts an' its great bloomin' eyes stare right at me. My hair stood on end I can tell you. And I shuts that door as fast as I can and locks and bolts it. The fair had come to the waste ground and it was one of them fair horses and it had pulled the stake out of the ground and gone walkabouts. I goes back upstairs and you could hear it going back up the drive dragging its chain behind it.'

'Did it ever come back?' asked younger brother.

'Now that's enough. You'll have them awake all night,' said mum.

That night I went to sleep in the saggy, damp bed, head to toe with my two younger brothers (two older brothers were in the other bed). Thoughts of playing on the beach and paddling in the sea, accompanied by the endless drumming of rain on the roof, lulled me into uneasy dreams of pennies cascading out of fruit machines, crabs crawling from the incoming sea to nip at my toes and a white horse forcing its way through the Helensolme door and clumping into our bedroom.

We woke the following morning to bright sunshine and a perfect blue sky. By the time we had finished breakfast it was quite hot. Gathering towels, swimming costumes, beach balls, buckets and spades, cricket equipment and sun tan lotion, we set off for the beach. We had pestered endlessly about this and now we were on our way. Leaving the camp behind, we passed the Amusement Arcade, went through the wooden level crossing gate and crossed the railway track. It was only some time later that we found out that at least two or three holiday makers, every year, were hit by trains on this level crossing.

Following the well-trodden path across the field and past an ice cream van, we came to the rusted, old railway track which ran at the foot of the concrete sea wall. We climbed the steps, inset into this lower wall, until we stood on the walkway with the upper wall above. Leaning on the upper wall (if you were an adult) or scrabbling up it (if you were a child) you could look out onto the beach and the Irish Sea. The tide was out. A breeze blew strongly from the sea. There was a sloping concrete platform which gave way to a stretch of duck pebbles. Beyond the pebbles was a stretch of sand. Grey - brown, low rollers washed forwards and backwards across the sand. We couldn't wait to get changed and dash to the sea.

Camping at the foot of the lower wall, protected from the coastal breeze, we changed into swimming gear. In those days we didn't, as any sensible person would, put costumes on beneath our clothes. No! It'd seemed part of the ritual to change in public view, negotiating clothes and towels - Houdini fashion! Towels around the waist, tugging at trousers and underclothing, we hopped about as if standing on hot coals. Of course, as soon as we reached for swimming trunks, desperately holding the towel in place, some older brother would pull at it, trying to expose your natural credentials to the world at large. There was much shouting, screaming, protesting and laughing. Wriggling and pulling and squirming, we eventually got our swimming trunks on and dropped the towels. Standing in line, we all wore traditional cut leg trunks apart from youngest brother. He stood there sheepishly in his navy blue, all - in - one, woollen, knitted costume looking like some strongman in a Victorian circus.

Nivea sun cream was dabbed on each one of us. Eldest brother who had taken up body - building, daubed olive oil on his already tanned body. He sat against the wall in a pose to show off his rippling muscles.

Hurriedly, we clambered up the sea wall steps and over the top of the upper wall so that we could race down to the sea. My father was in close attendance, shouting at us to slow down. He needn't have worried. We came to the bank of pebbles. Barefoot, we picked our way over the pebbles, hopping and squealing. It was then that I realized why so many people were wearing blue, white and pink plastic sandals. But then we reached the comfort of the soft, warm sand. Whooping and hollering, we raced down to the sea, splashing through warm channels of water, left behind by the receding tide. We raced ankle deep into the sea and raced out again. We jumped over small waves. We paddled along the edge. Then, one year older brother suddenly dashed into the water and dived into a breaking wave. When he surfaced and stood up, waist deep, he cried, 'Come on in, you scardies! Water's lovely and warm.'

Gingerly and steadily, we all waded out. Already my father was a bit further out, swimming around. With many an oooh and aaah, we inched deeper and deeper. But then, of course, came the obligatory splashing from one year older brother. We screamed and shouted and then submerged ourselves to avoid further torture. After splashing and swimming and jumping in off each other's shoulders, we came out of the water to dig a hole and build a dam. As we knelt down to scrape at the sand with our hands, one year older brother was suddenly pointing and laughing uncontrollably. Looking up, we could see youngest brother just standing there forlornly. Water was cascading from him and the woollen, one piece hung down below his knees, stretched by the weight of the water. As he moved towards us the costume bounced up and down and a gush of water ran from his gusset down his legs. We could hear him moaning as he waddled back towards the pebbles and the sea wall.

The sun beat down. We ran back to the sea wall and sat with backs to the wall and legs outstretched, pointing towards the rusted, disused railway track. It was now very hot. Ice creams all round failed to cool us. More cream had been applied. Then it was back to the sea and then back to the sea wall for ham and cheese buns and a swig of Dandelion and Burdock. Then back to the beach. And so it went on all afternoon.

Later that evening, back at Helensolme, one year older brother clapped me on the shoulder, saying, 'Are you coming for a game of cricket?' I shrieked out loud.

'What on earth's the matter?' asked my mother, turning from the table where she was cutting peeled potatoes into big, fat chips and dropping them into a bowl of water.

'Ow! It's my shoulder! He's hitting my sore shoulder!'

With that mother made me take off my T- shirt. I was bright red all over.

'Oh, that is sore! You're well and truly sun burnt. I told you - all of you - to keep putting the cream on. Come here! You need calamine lotion.'

She examined my other two brothers, one year younger and one year older and they, too, were sun burnt. All three of us were daubed with the pink calamine lotion. Youngest brother stood, watching smugly. He was untouched - protected by his all-in-one, woollen bathing suit.

All through the evening, at night in bed, and for the next few days, complaints of: 'Ow! That's my sun burn!' could be heard. We spent the rest of the week playing and swimming with T-shirts on.

On the Friday, our last day, a small catastrophe occurred. We were all in the sea and my father had been hoisting us, with both hands linked, up and over his shoulder, so that we dived into the waves behind him. Then he dived under himself. Resurfacing he stood, looking bewildered, with his bottom lip sucked into his mouth. He looked like a turtle opening and closing its mouth.

'Gugger, gugger! Mo feef, mo feef! Uv goh! Inv arter! Loch! Loch!'

Not understanding a word, we just stood staring at him. Then he opened his mouth and pointed. He had no teeth. His false teeth had come out in his last dive and now lay on the bed of the Irish Sea. He dived below the surface and came up. Shaking his head, he dived again, kicking his legs frantically and splashing water everywhere. Surfacing again, he shouted, ''Um on! 'Ep me vind mo feef!'

We all dived and tried to reach the bottom, peering into the dirty, brown water. Then one year old brother told youngest brother to run and fetch eldest brother. We all continued to search. Eldest brother arrived and it was his superior underwater swimming technique which finally won the day. Triumphantly, he emerged from the waves, one arm raised and brandishing a lower set of teeth and in the other a matching upper set of teeth.

The next day our first real holiday was over. We would remember that holiday with fondness and happiness…hill-billy shack, sun burn, false teeth and all.

2. From Grasmere to the World

After I had passed the Eleven Plus exam and started to go to Grammar School, my travel horizons began to widen. There was a school holiday to the Lake District and I was allowed to go. To Grasmere, to be precise.

And so, during the Whit holiday, a party of boys ranging from first years to sixth formers, along with various masters, set out in minibuses. Our holiday billet was not a hotel, not even a Youth Hostel, but the Grasmere Village Hall, next to Broadgate Park. We all took our kitbags, rucksacks, holdalls, cases, into the hall and were given sleeping quarters. Lower School had the corridor down the right hand side of the hall, Middle School, the left hand side corridor and Upper School, the stage and its wings. Masters occupied various small rooms off the hall.

As we laid claim to our sleeping spaces, everyone unpacked and rolled out their sleeping bags, laying claim to their territorial rights. Everyone except me. With a large family, my parents could not afford a sleeping bag. So I unrolled my blankets. I had two grey - brown, heavy duty, army surplus blankets joined down both sides and one end with large, bright red, woollen stitches. I looked down the line at the row of quilted blue, green and red sleeping bags. No one else had a homemade sleeping bag. I just waited for someone to point at my blankets and for everyone to laugh. But I was saved by King Kong. King Kong, shortened to the nickname Kong, was the strict and ferocious French master. He was an imposing figure, with bald head, a hooked nose and beady eyes which never missed anything. Back at school, he would pounce on unsuspecting boys for the slightest misdemeanour. If a master let you out of his lesson late and you walked to your next classroom along the quadrangle and past his room, he would pounce. His classroom door would be flung open. You would freeze on the spot.

'Boy, you are late!' he would snarl. 'Disturbing my lesson, I will not have!Report to me at break!'

You would scuttle off to your next lesson in the certain knowledge that, at break, you would receive three strokes on the backside with his dreaded white, tennis pump. We all knew and understood that on holiday he would not act any differently.

Now he loomed in front of us.

'Now boys, listen carefully.' There was a sudden silence, all except for one boy who continued to chat to his friend.

'Isherwood! What did I just say? I said listen, boy!'

Isherwood was a born victim. He always did the wrong thing at the wrong time. More than anyone else, Isherwood had felt the wrath of Kong, felt the imprint of the tennis pump on his backside.

'You will roll up your sleeping bags, place them neatly against the wall with your luggage next to them. Then you will all proceed quietly into the main hall. This part of the holiday is very important. There are rules for how you conduct yourself in this Hall, in the village and out on the Fells. You will listen carefully and make sure you abide by all the rules.'

Very quickly I rolled up my "sleeping bag" and put it against the wall with my brown holdall.

In the Hall we were put into groups. Each group went on their selected Fell Walk each day, except on their Duty Day. On that day the Duty Group had to prepare packed lunches for the walking groups, peel potatoes, wash and chop vegetables and generally prepare the evening meal. We were told that "lights out" was at ten o'clock and everyone had to be settled at that time. For the rest of the afternoon we were free to explore our surroundings while the sixth form group prepared our first evening meal. We played football in the park and, with a small group of friends, I scrambled up and down the roche moutonnee. After a while a master came into the park and blew a whistle. We all gathered round and were taken, in a long line, supervised by the master and three sixth form prefects, to Grasmere village. We visited the grave of William Wordsworth in the graveyard of St.

Oswald's church and had a look inside the church itself. Then we were given "free time" and told to meet in one hour's time on the bridge over the River Rothay, next to the church. We shouted excitedly at the shoals of fish flitting under the bridge and languishing in the quiet, deep pool on the inside bend where the river gently looped around the Riverside Café. We went onto the Riverside Café. Sitting outside with my friends, on the terrace overhanging the river, I had a strawberry milkshake which had a scoop of vanilla ice cream in it. Warm sunshine glinting on the translucent water, still and lazy, except when the ducks chased each other, delicious milkshake the like of which I had never tasted before, the cry of hooded crows swooping from the grey, ivied towers of St. Oswald's, all lulled me into a trance like state. Never before had I experienced such beauty and tranquility. Then we looked around some shops for postcards to send home ending up at Sarah Nelson's Gingerbread Shop, snuggled into the wall by the church gate. It had once been the small schoolroom where William Wordsworth had taught. Nibbling on a gingerbread man we went back to the bridge and walked back to the Village Hall.

Trestle tables had been set up in the main hall and we all sat and ate the prepared meal of boiled potatoes, cabbage and stew. After indoor games or further football in the park we all trooped in to get ready for bedtime. Buckets of cold water outside on the gravel were used for a quick wash and brushing of teeth. Soon everyone was in pyjamas sitting on sleeping bags, chatting or playing cards. It wasn't long before monitors and prefects (sent by the masters) came along the corridors saying, 'Anyone for toilets. Go now! Then everyone into sleeping bags. Everything away. It's time for lights out.'

"Anyone for toilets" was, of course, nearly everyone. But, finally, everyone was settled into their sleeping bags. The lights went out. There was tittering and shouting and ghost noises. Then torches were switched on and flashed down the corridor, along walls and across ceilings.

'I bet Smithy's got his teddy bear,' shouted Flog Fairhurst. Boys whistled and jeered.

Then we heard the voice of Kong. 'This will not do! This is your first, last and only warning. Torches must be put away. This is not the time to use them. Any torch being misused will be confiscated. Any more noises and the culprits will be punished. Goodnight!'

A few voices returned the "goodnight" then all was a hush as we listened for Kong's retreating footsteps.

Then there was whispering and quiet tittering. All went quiet for a short while. Then Flog Fairhurst's voice broke in:

'Banksy! You dirty bugger! Farting in my face! Whatta pong!' There were howls of laughter. And someone said, "Shush!" But Isherwood was never one to heed a warning. He was on his feet dancing along the corridor. With his torch under his chin, lighting up his face, he began to sing, 'I'm King Kong and I sing a song, and saying put your torches away …'

Torchlight suddenly beamed from behind him.

'Isherwood!' said an angry voice. 'You disobedient boy! Come with me into the hall!'

Isherwood's torch was taken from him and he was marched into the hall. Seconds later three large thuds and groans were heard. Isherwood hopped back into the corridor clutching his buttocks, wincing and sobbing. He climbed straight into his sleeping bag and lay down sobbing quietly. Following him, legs apart, arms akimbo, Kong stood clutching the white tennis pump.

'There will be no more nonsense tonight! The next boy will receive the same and will be removed to sleep somewhere in isolation!'

He marched off back to his quarters.

No one spoke. Then, in the darkness, a harsh whisper said, 'The bloody, fat Frog maniac! It's not right! We're on holiday! We'll have to put a stop to this!'

Everyone looked into the darkness, listening and holding their breath. We couldn't see who said it but we all knew it was Flog Fairhurst. Then all was silence.

The following morning at breakfast Flog Fairhurst was chuntering to everyone on his table.

'You'll see! I'll stop that bugger! Wait 'til we get back. We'll have those bloody white pumps!'

Everyone hitched rucksacks onto their backs and put on woolly climbing socks and walking boots. I didn't have any walking boots. I donned my indestructible school shoes. They were bought by my father from Pilkington's Glass Works where he worked. They were safety shoes. They had thick, green soles and bright orange uppers which ended in steel toe caps. They were meant to last the duration of my school life. And they did! I used to kick walls and kerbs and anything solid at school to damage and wear them out. I even dropped half bricks on them. But they were indestructible. However, at break times, I was always picked one of the first for any football side. One tackle from my steel toe caps and the poor unfortunate recipient would be lame for weeks. I was always given a wide berth and once I hit a shot with them, the ball flew like a missile through the goals.

Our party was headed for Helvellyn. We climbed quite steeply in warm sunshine but even as we trudged up the spine of Swirral Edge clouds were suddenly swirling around the summit. Once on top we had wonderful views of Red Tarn below, Thirlmere, Ullswater, Grasmere, and all the surrounding peaks. But the air grew colder and, in a matter of five minutes, the mist had closed in obscuring most of the vista. We ate our packed lunches crouched and sat behind the dry stone wall shelter. The masters in charge began to look anxious and hurriedly gathered everyone together. Waterproof anoraks were donned; in my case a plastic pack-a-mack.

As we started back down Swirral Edge the mist thickened and we could only see yards in front of us. One of the masters stopped and brought out his compass. He told us to walk carefully in single file and we picked our way, somewhat apprehensively and tentatively, down the Edge until, at last, after what seemed an age, we emerged out of the cloud.

Once back down it was warm and sunny again. Arriving back at the Hall at three p.m. we had free time before the evening meal. It was then that Flog Fairhurst's daring plan was revealed. Gathering together all the Lower School boys who had returned from their treks on the grass below the roche moutonnee, he made a rousing speech.

'We're all together in this! Right!' There were shouts of agreement. 'He'll not give anyone else three of the best with those white pumps of his 'cos we're gonna take them. Right!' Cheers rang out. 'His group's not back yet. So I'm going into his room to get them! I need a few of you to keep watch. Then we all march down the village to dispose of them.'

Three or four boys stood at various stations keeping watch. Flog Fairhurst disappeared into Kong's small room near the front entrance of the Hall. When he came out again he held two white tennis shoes triumphantly above his head. In one large mob we marched into the village. Passing the church we stopped on the bridge over the river. There, Flog Fairhurst flung the tennis shoes into the water. There was cheering, laughter and shouts of triumph as the current swept the two pumps along and under the bridge.

Whether Kong ever suspected what had happened I don't know. But he did not carry out any inquisition over the matter and no one else received three strokes of the pump during the rest of our stay.

The euphoria of the ceremonial "baptism of the white pumps" was soon to fall flat the very next day. It was a glorious sunny day; unblemished blue sky and hot sun. The day on which tragedy struck.

Our party went up to Easedale Tarn. We stopped at Sour Milk Ghyll and sat on the grassy ledge at the other side of the deep, green-translucent plunge pool. It was a beautiful day. The sky was endlessly blue and the spray from the waterfall cooled us down. Continuing on, we reached the Tarn where we spent some time skimming pebbles across the dark surface, paddling in the icy water and eating our packed lunches. We walked around the edge of the tarn up to Blea Crag. Here, we turned back, walked round the Tarn and descended into Far Easedale Gill at the other side of the Tarn and dropped down back into Grasmere village.

Sweeping into the Hall, we were in high spirits, looking forward to the free time out in the sunshine. Talking excitedly, we rushed into the Main Hall only to stop suddenly in our tracks. Boys and masters were stood or sat against the wall in silence. Some boys were sobbing and the masters were grim faced. Mr. Norsley, Kong, stepped forward, hand held up like a policemen on point duty. In his softest, quietest voice he said, 'Boys please be quiet. Come over here and sit down.' Then he cleared his throat and swallowed.

'You're the last group back and you need to know what happened today. I'm sorry to have to break the sad news that one of our boys - today…' There was moisture welling in the corner of his eyes. '…today - one of your fellow pupils…has drowned…' We all sat down in silent disbelief.

Coming over the top of Loughrigg the group of Middle School boys had descended to the tarn. Loughrigg Tarn is a particularly beautiful, almost circular tarn with dazzling waters. It must have looked so inviting on a tranquil, sunny day such as that one. Loughrigg itself would have been reflected in its calm waters and across those waters it would have presented a stunning view to the North West of the rugged profile of the Langdale Pikes. Because they were hot the masters had allowed the boys to swim in the tarn. One boy got out of his depth and drowned. If you visit Loughrigg Tarn today and walk around it to a small, grassy spur by the water's edge backed by the green slopes of Loughrigg itself, you will find a small, wooden cross with a brass plaque on it. It bears the words, *In Memory of... (The* boy's name) *Drowned 4th June 1960 whilst on Holiday with Cowley Boys Grammar School.* This, of course, saddened everybody and took the joy out of the holiday. We all went to a special service at the small Methodist church on College Street. The boy, himself, was a quiet, popular boy, who was always considerate to others. This was the saddest holiday I've ever been on and one I will never forget.

---oOo---

Beyond this, throughout my youth, I never really went on any holidays or travelled much. My next real foray into the unknown was my honeymoon. Getting married on 21st. December, we travelled down to London for four days of honeymooning. Signing the hotel register I wrote, "Mr. Allan Bate and Miss Ann Roughley" but no eyebrows were raised as I bent forward and confetti cascaded onto the Reception desk. We soon found that, in 1968, London was closed for Christmas. That evening we did find one dining establishment – aWimpey's Burger Bar.

Other early travels came as we reared our young family. Staying in the father-in-law's caravan at Combe Martin in North Devon gave us many years of happy family holidays. There were two memorable incidents. One was when oldest son, Steven, at eighteen months first saw the sea on Combe Martin beach. In the blink of an eye he had dashed headlong to the edge of the water. But he did not stop. I was up to my knees, fully clothed, before I gathered him up. Another was when my youngest son, Stuart, then eight months old, sat one hot, sunny afternoon playing in a small stream running through the pebble bank on Newberry Beach and down to the sea. We did not realize that there was a problem until he began to shiver, then turn purple, then turn black. Whipping him up to the site we were able to sit him in a warm bath and he gradually recovered.

Later we bought our own static caravan on a site near Levens Hall in the Lake District. It was close to the embankment of the River Kent. We had many happy holidays there including the time when both boys had taken a dingy onto the river, got fed up and decided to play on the bank. They appeared on the top of the embankment covered in black mud, only the whites of their eyes peering out. As the children grew older we extended our horizons – the then Yugoslavia, Sorrento, Riva on Lake Garda, Florida. Then they began to travel independently and so did we.

3. Mike's Underpants

As independent travellers (without children), our trip to Venice began problematically. We had arranged to go on the trip with two long standing friends, Mike and Margaret. Just a week before our departure date airport workers at Italian airports had gone on strike. We were advised that there could be problems especially with flight cancellations. Our flight was booked from Stansted to Treviso. Mike had booked a small bed and breakfast place close to the Rialto Bridge. If we could not fly we would lose our money on this accommodation. So, with a week to go, Mike had cancelled the bed and breakfast place and we agreed that we would wait until the day to find out if the flight was still going.

On the morning of our departure we found that the flight was still scheduled. Arriving at our house at twelve noon, Mike had agreed that we should access the internet and find fresh accommodation. Our departure time was at six in the evening. So we booked rooms at the Ambassador Tre Rui which was not far from St. Mark's Square.

Later that night, at ten o'clock, we arrived at Treviso airport. In the small airport foyer we bought tickets for the ATVO Eurobus for 9 euros return (5 euros single). We boarded the bus in heavy rain and settled back for the one and a half hour journey to Venice.

At eleven thirty the bus crossed the Ponte Della Liberta and stopped at the bus terminal in Piazzale Roma. By now the rain was torrential and we hurried across the Piazzale pulling cases behind us and heading in the direction of the Grand Canal. Buying tickets for the vaporetto from a small kiosk we dropped down steps and dashed under the shelter at the waterbus stop. We boarded the vaporetto, at this time of the night, with only two other people.

Chugging down the Grand Canal we approached the Ponte di Rialto. At the other side of Ponte di Rialto we disembarked at the next waterbus stop. Rain fell heavily. We splashed through puddles and sheltered in a doorway to study the wet rag of a map which hung from Mike's hand. On the map we found our destination - Calle dei Fabbri. The rain fell in sheets and, as it was now midnight, we desperately wanted to reach our accommodation. Trudging and splashing along the Riva del Carron we soon came to Calle dei Fabbri. We hurried, heads down through the narrow calle until, at last, we arrived at the Ambassador Tre

Rui. Reporting to the Reception Desk we were told that there were no available rooms and that we had been transferred to the Hotel Royal San Marco which was just a bit further along Calle dei Fabbri.

  Indeed, after a short walk, we reached the small, glass fronted entrance to the Royal San Marco. It was like a shop window. We stepped into a small, dimly lit vestibule. A dummy in long silk, Venetian robes stared out at us from behind a white plastic mask, looking something akin to the Phantom of The Opera. An arrow indicated that Reception was up a flight of stairs. Dripping wet and panting with the exertion of lugging cases up the stairs, we reached the Reception Desk. On dinging the bell the tall, lean desk man appeared from a small room behind. Checking in, we were informed that we were on the sixth floor but the lift only went to the fourth and then we would have to use the stairs. On the fourth floor we struggled with the cases up a wobbling, open tread staircase. We were confronted with two small rooms. Once inside we just stood and stared. Bottle green lino tiles did nothing to enhance the mucky, cream petition walls. Two single beds cringed in one corner. Portable camp beds looked more comfortable than these. There was a musky smell of damp. The narrow bathroom was only accessible by sliding through the doorway; the door couldn't fully open as it was stopped by the toilet bowl. Once through you had to close the door to be able to use either the shower or the toilet. Filthy, grime ridden, mildewed tiles clung to the wall. As we walked out into the corridor to go to Mike and Margaret's room, they were approaching our room. With shaking heads and despondent faces, we met in the middle. On inspecting their room it, too, followed the design of a portable toilet. Nuns' cells would be far more luxurious and comfortable.

Minutes later we were back at Reception with cases and belongings.

'We're not staying in those rooms!' I said.

'We paid 700 euros and we should be in the Ambassador Tre Rui. We don't want the rooms!' said Mike.

The Italian receptionist did not register any surprise or make any objection. He seemed to understand instantly and, without more ado, he picked up the phone and spoke to someone briefly.

'I have made for you two rooms in Hotel San Marco. It is sister hotel. Come, I show you. It is near on Calle.'

He took us across the Calle dei Fabbri to the Best Western Hotel San Marco. It was close to a small bridge over a narrow canal which led to Sottoportego opening onto the Piazza San Marco.

That night we slept in the eaves of the hotel in a room cramped with a king sized bed and with a small balcony which overlooked roof tops and dark alleys and spaces between the buildings. But, at least, it was clean and comfortable. That night the rain battered against the skylight above, lightning flashed intermittently and thunder cracked and rumbled.

At 7 a.m. the following morning the bells of the Campanile San Marco woke us, closely followed by the sirens. Half asleep, half awake, my immediate thoughts were of a wartime bombing raid. Then I realised it was the normal Venice warning of rising water. After breakfast we got ready for our first foray into Venice.

As Mike was busy packing, repacking and checking his rucksack (something he was well known for), we went outside to get our bearings. Looking up the Calle to the left, we were amused to see local shopkeepers making ready for the day. Carrying goods into their shops they waded, in wellingtons, through the flooded Calle. Porters, in waders, rounded the bend, pulling trolleys loaded with boxes through the knee deep water. Outside the doors of Hotel San Marco, we stood on an island of dry land where the road sloped upwards towards the bridge over the canal. Walking to my right and planting myself on the small hump backed bridge leading towards Sottoportego, I looked towards the tunnelled entrance into St. Mark's Square. It, too, was completely flooded. Some Americans standing next to us had taped white plastic bags over their shoes and set off wading through the water to our left, disappearing with raucous laughter round the bend. Running back inside, we met Mike and Margaret emerging from the lift.

'Marooned! We're marooned!' I shouted, sounding like Private Fraser in Dad's Army.

Mike and Margaret laughed and thought we were joking until they stepped outside and realized that we were, indeed, marooned. Just then a porter rounded the corner pulling his trolley. Another man stood on the trolley, hitching a lift.

'Blimey,' said Mike, having popped onto the bridge to see that the entrance to St. Mark's was also cut off by flood water. 'You're right, we're marooned!'

Various suggestions to beat the flood were offered. Plastic bags "a l'Americans"; but we hadn't got any. Piggy backs for the ladies; but confidence in the ability and strength of the male pack horses was non – existent. Trying to hail a porter's trolley for a lift; but at that moment there seemed to be a dearth and sufficient knowledge of the Italian was lacking. Relaxing in the hotel until the flood had subsided was not favoured in that our stay was only for four nights and there was so much to see and do in that time.

It was then that the inventive and irrepressible nature of Mike came to the fore.

'Wellies! That's what we need! Wellies!' The most obvious and simplest solutions to problems are always the ones that work best. But we had not packed any wellingtons. Not to be deterred Mike continued, 'The shops are open. Knowing about this flooding which happens frequently, there must be plenty of shops selling wellingtons. We've just got to go and buy some.'

Everyone else stood, shaking their heads, knowing that to get to such shops, we needed to get across the floods. But Mike was in no mood to concede defeat.

'Right! I'll go off and wade through the water and find a shop. Then I'll bring the wellies back.' Already, he had taken off his shoes and socks and handed them to Margaret. He was rolling his trousers up to his knees. 'Now, what sizes do we need? I'm nines, Margaret's sixes...'

Having ascertained our sizes, he set off, looking back, mumbling, 'Ann, fives...Margaret, sixes...Allan, eights...Mike, nines. What are those in continental sizes?'

Fifteen minutes later, Mike returned without a single wellington in hand or an olive leaf in his mouth. Mission Impossible had not been accomplished. Mike had found wellingtons galore but, with a stranded, captive market, the cheapest Mike could find cost 12 euros a pair. And so, all four of us, carrying shoes and socks in hands, and with trousers rolled up to the knee, set off wading along Calle dei Fabbri in the direction of the Rialto Bridge.

After a short while we turned right into the Campo San Salvador. With wet feet, we strode into the Campo, which, being higher was a haven of dryness. Crossing the Campo, we headed to the sanctuary of the Chiesa San Salvatore. In the dim light of the small church we soon realized that we were the only ones there. We sat on a pew with wet feet. Ann used her innate initiative as we other three sat down on the nearest pew. Hopping from foot to foot, she dried her feet on the dark blue curtains which were a screen in front of the nave of the church. Bending over, Mike rooted in his rucksack, apparently a familiar tendency when he was on holiday or a walk. A tendency which had frequently annoyed his eldest son in times past. However, after what seemed like a few minutes of rummaging, he cried out triumphantly waving underwear in the air; a pair of green checked Debenham's boxer shorts to be exact. His habit of packing a spare pair of boxer shorts in case of emergencies proved to be a real winner, as me, Mike and Margaret dried our feet on them. Then, fully shod again, we set off on our exploration of Venice.

As the morning wore on duckboards had been put in place and water was subsiding. We went to Canareggio, the Jewish Ghetto. In the open air market we saw every type of mushroom on display and artichoke hearts in bowls of water. Then, there were liqueurs on display each with a scene from the Kama Sutra, Soixante Neuf featuring regularly. We had lunch at Restaurant Vesuvio where we ate beautiful pizzas. We took in the striking balcony view on the edge of the Grand Canal from C'an D'or Palace.

In the few following days, we visited, by vaporetto, the islands of Murano, Torcello and Burano. We particularly liked the pretty stucco – fronted houses along the canal in the fishing village of Burano. These were painted in pastel shades of pink, beige, purple, green, yellow, blue and lilac. We enjoyed a delicious lunch at the Caffe Vecchio on the edge of Piazza Baldassore Galuppi.

The following day we were relieved to find that the flooding had subsided. We visited all the usual haunts – St. Mark's Square and Basilica, the Doge's Palace and The Bridge of Sighs. On visiting Ponte di Rialto we came across the Chiesa di San Giacometto, with its distinctive façade clock and bell tower. The church was traditionally considered to be the oldest in Venice dating from the fifth century and having been rebuilt several times. That very evening an ensemble was performing some of the works of Vivaldi, Mozart, Paschelbel and Albinoni. Buying tickets for this performance at 20:45 at a cost of 18.50 euros, we went on our way.

The evening came and we set off towards Ponte di Rialto for a pre-concert dinner. Crossing the bridge, we turned down left onto the canal side and down a narrow alleyway which led to the Trattoria alla Madonna in Calle de la Madonna. The restaurant was brimming with local Italians and we enjoyed an excellent meal.

Arriving at the Chiesa di San Giacometto we were a little late and all the pews were already full. A lady escorted us down to the very front to five chairs just at the side of the altar steps. Already seated was a very smartly dressed, elderly Italian gentleman. He wore a light coloured suit with collar and tie. We sat in the four seats next to him.

The four musicians were already assembled and very soon a hush fell over the church and the performance began. They had been chosen from the best known Italian music schools. Throughout the performance the elegant, elderly gentleman made notes in a small, hand sized pad. Every so often he would frown, shake his head from side to side and tutt. At the end of each piece, he did not applaud and, when the performance was over, he stood up, put the notepad and pen into his inside jacket pocket and marched unceremoniously down the aisle and out of the church. If he was a classical music critic then he wasn't very impressed, even though we and the rest of the audience were most appreciative.

---oOo---

It was on another memorable occasion that Mike's underpants came to the rescue. Having reached the pier at Glenridding, we clambered aboard the steamer to travel up Ullswater in the Lake District to Howtown. From here we would walk back along the opposite shore of Ullswater, a six mile hike back to Glenridding. But, earlier, it had rained. Once aboard we found that all the wooden seats were wet. Like a conjuror, Mike pulled out his famous spare boxer shorts from the depths of his rucksack. Having wiped four seats dry we duly sat down. Other passengers stood for the duration of the journey, occasionally staring at us in the disbelief that we would sit on wet seats.

Thus originated the well-known adage: "Problems can always be solved with a pair of Mike's underpants."

4. Kettles, Keys, Kerfuffle, Kerkyra and Kamikaze

Travel and holidays don't always match up to expectations. Locations are not always those of your imagination. Events sometimes creep up on you without warning. Catastrophe is always looming, awaiting some unforeseen chance to descend. That is when experiences become memorable and leave an indelible scar on your psyche.

One such stay in Portugal was the source of two of the aforementioned mishaps. A fortnight's holiday to Praia da Rocha in the Algarve will long be remembered for *The Case of the Boiling Kettle* and *The Case of the Lost Keys*. We arrived in Praia da Rocha with Friends Joe and Sylvia, two teenage boys and one teenage girl. We settled into our separate rooms on the fifth floor of the apartment block.

Things went well. We visited the pretty marina at Vilamoura, had a lunch of freshly grilled sardines and chilled Vino Verdi on the dockside at Portimao and went to Lagos.

Then, one evening we visited an up market restaurant set on a terrace with its own small outdoor swimming pool, overlooking a sandy cove illuminated with pretty lights. It was a barmy evening and we enjoyed the local fare and wine. I had grilled turbot and all seemed well with the world. The following morning we took to the sun on the sands of Praia da Rocha, overlooked by the russet cliff line. It was at lunchtime that I felt a little queasy and only had a drink at a local café. Returning to our apartment after a lazy afternoon, we rested up. I was beginning to feel hot and flushed and aching all over. Later, as we began to get ready to go out for dinner, I suddenly felt much worse. Between being sick several times and taking to my bed, the two teenage boys went out to dine by themselves in a local café where they could get what they considered was gourmet food – beef burger and chips. Then I began to feel hot and sweaty and shivered with cold alternately. Eventually my wife boiled water in the metal kettle on the cooker rings to make me a cup of Hot Lemon. I say eventually because the cooker kept activating the trip switch and she had to reset it several times. When our friends called from across the corridor I was still prostrate in the bedroom feeling very sorry for myself. I informed them that I felt too ill to go out and that, even the thought of food made me feel worse. And so it was decided that their enjoyment should not be affected and they went to dine without me.

At first I drifted into a shallow sleep but after a while I became restless and irritated. I began to sweat profusely and I was becoming hotter and hotter. My body temperature seemed to be soaring; I felt weak and dizzy; I was choking and gasping for breath. In the end I slid off the bed and staggered through the open bedroom door into the kitchen and living room. A fog of steam hit me. The whole room was filled with this swirling mist. I was beginning to panic. Had delirium set in? Was I about to pass out? Was the room on fire? Then I noticed the glowing ring on the cooker on which the kettle was still standing. Quickly I turned the ring off. Foolishly I went to grab the kettle but winced and drew back as the hot handle burnt my hand. Once I had held my hand under a cold water tap, I adopted a more sensible strategy. Using a tea towel, I grasped the kettle handle to pick it up. It didn't seem to move. It was as if it was stuck down. Then, tugging strongly, I pulled it off the electric ring and held it aloft. The kettle was bottomless! The bottom had completely melted and was spread over the cooker ring. I opened windows and, as the fog dispersed and the temperature dropped, I felt a lot better. Because the switch had tripped and the electric ring had gone off, when the trip switch had been reset the ring was no longer glowing but the cooker knob was still set to "on".

- - - o O o - - -

The Case of the Lost Keys occurred later in the holiday. We had hired cars at the airport. Albufeira, the Monchique Mountains, Alvore, were some of the places that we visited. On the day that the teenagers wished to spend time in

Praia da Rocha we decided to go to Carvoeiro. Arriving at Carvoeiro, a sandy cove between two rocky headlands, I found it almost impossible to find a parking space. So we drove on up the steep road winding up out of Carvoeiro. Not far along this road we came to a beautiful rocky inlet. Waves had cut an archway through the cliff and the sea ran into a deep creek between smooth, rocky banks. Spying the beautiful, deep turquoise channel with people sunbathing and swimming, the temptation was too great for me. Slowing down we could see that there was a small car park adjacent to it. As if starting from pole position in a Formula One Grand Prix race, I accelerated into a vacant space. Down to the left a footpath led to a bridge spanning another inlet. At the other side of the bridge was a café. Once out of the car, I turned to look longingly at the inviting water of the inlet.

'Go on, if you're going. I know you want to get in there,' said my wife, Ann. 'We'll sit in the sun on these rocks.'

I couldn't wait. Fortunately, I was wearing swim shorts. Within seconds I'd balanced myself on the edge of a round, smooth rock and dived in. The water was clear and warm. I surfaced, dived again and then swam along the channel to the rock archway. Then, submerging, I swam underwater back along the channel. Resting momentarily on the edge of a rock, I looked down into the clear turquoise depths. I just had to see how deep it was. With a surface dive that a dolphin would have been proud of, I swam down deeper and deeper. At this point the inlet must have been about twenty feet deep. Down and down I went until I touched the large rounded boulders on the bed of the channel. Holding my breath I surfaced again quickly. I swam and dived for another five minutes. Having satisfied my urge, I then clambered up onto the rocks where my wife was waiting with a towel. Once dried, we made our way back to the car. After standing by the car for half a minute, I began to get impatient.

'Well, are you going to open up the car or not?'

'I can't,' retorted Ann.

'Can't? What do you mean?'

'I can't because you've got the keys.'

'I haven't. I gave them to you.'

'No, you didn't. You put them in your…'

It was then that I realised that I had put the keys into my swim short's pocket. Patting the pockets and then frantically plunging a hand into each one, I discovered that they were empty. Four of us stood there, open mouthed, as the realisation of what had happened dawned on us. Immediately I was back in the water performing multiple surface dives to swim down to the bed of the channel searching frantically for a set of car keys. Having surfaced for the umpteenth time, other swimmers became intrigued by my dolphin impersonation. Soon, groups of English, Portuguese, French and Spanish swimmers were diving down into the depths of the rocky channel. But it was all in vain. It didn't take me long to realise that the keys would have slipped down into the gaps between the large rounded pebbles and boulders on the bed of the channel.

Dripping, and somewhat sheepishly, I clambered out of the water and picked my way over the rocks towards my wife and friends. Their stern, resolute stances and exasperated expressions told me everything I needed to know.

'No keys. Stuck here. What do we do now?' said Ann.

'Well…er…we'll have to get some keys…' I began.

'The car rental's office number is etched on the rear windscreen,' said friend Joe. 'We'd better ring them. Perhaps they'll send out spare keys to us.'

This was pre-mobile phone use. So, the two ladies set off for the café whilst Joe and I set off to find a public phone. After a long walk back into Carvoeiro we made the phone call. Yes, they had spare keys. No, they could not bring them out. We had to go there, back to Praia da Rocha, and we would be charged the equivalent of £6 for the keys. Returning to the ladies in the café, we explained the situation. It now meant a taxi journey to the car rental office and back.

Two hours later we were back, armed with the spare car keys. It was a silent journey back to our apartment in Praia da Rocha.

---oOo---

Another mishap, misadventure or kerfuffle took place nearer to home. On holiday in the Lake District, my wife and I drove to Seatoller in Borrowdale. Parking at the National Trust car park at Seatoller Barn, we set off to conquer Castle Crag.

After leaving the B5289, we set off up an ascending track. An easy walk took us along a fairly level track following the contours of the fell side. We passed over footbridges at Scaleclose Gill, Tongue Gill and then forded Lavery Gill. At this time it was cloudy but dry and the wind was getting stronger. Leaving the track, we reached a short, grassy plateau and bore left round a rocky outcrop. With Castle Crag in front of us we stopped on a shale pathway. Ann, my wife, took one look at the steep, slate spoil heap which girded the rocky outcrop leading to the summit of Castle Crag, and immediately made it clear that she would not be continuing any further. By now the wind was gusting strongly and she made assertions that maybe I should not be climbing up the spoil heap. But I hadn't come this far just to admire this summit which held the promise of a fantastic vista up and down Borrowdale. Castle Crag dominates "The Jaws of Borrowdale". Thousands of years ago its small but level summit was the site of an Iron Age hill fort. But during the last centuries it was quarried for its slate. Today there is a spoil heap of slate clinging to the outcrop of Castle Crag. A steep, zig – zagging path works its way through the cascade of loose slate to the summit.

So, it was decided that Ann would wait on the path and I would nip up to the top and back. With rucksack on my back containing the mobile phone, I set off with the parting comment that I would return to that spot in about ten minutes. The zig – zagging path up the slate scree was well defined and soon I had reached the top. Walking across the fat top, I visited the dry stone ramparts of the hill fort. Then I went to look at the slate plaque which was a poignant memorial to Lieutenant Hamer and the other Borrowdale men who died fighting for their country in the First World War. Placed at its foot were a couple of poppy wreaths and some small wooden crosses each one centred with a poppy. Crossing the flat summit, I reached the far edge where the wind was whipping across strongly. From here the views up Borrowdale towards Grange and Keswick were spectacular. The River Derwent wound its way majestically in the valley bottom.

Everything was fine until I came to descend the spoil heap. Reaching the edge again I looked for the zig – zagging path through the slate scree. From the bottom the path way was clear and distinct but suddenly looking down, I could not see any sign of it. Moving along the edge, I scanned the whole slate spoil heap. No matter where I went I could not see the pathway down. From above the whole spoil heap was just one smooth mass of slate. I had no idea where my point of exit from the pathway to the summit had been. Becoming impatient, I decided to descend the slate in the manner of scree walking. It was now very windy and there was rain in the air. I knew that Ann would be worrying. I knew that she would be panicking. Already in her mind I would have been blown from the summit. Sliding and slipping down the slate, I finally reached the grass slopes. However, on seeing the River Derwent down below I realised that I had come down the left hand side of the Crag and not the right side where I had climbed up. I was quite a little way down the mountain slope with a dry stone wall to my right and no sign of the plateau where I'd left Ann. It was then that I knew I had descended at the wrong side. So I began to clamber back up the grassy fell which led to another dry stone wall in the distance. Reaching the wall I climbed over the stile to find myself on another grassy slope which led to another dry stone wall. It was like being in that nightmare where you are trying to get to a destination which is always just out of your reach. I realised that time was passing and so I began to run and struggle up the slope. Eventually I clambered over a stile and there was the plateau. It was now raining. There was the plateau but, as I had feared and expected, my wife was not. Pulling up my anorak hood, I stood wondering, with the wind buffeting me and the rain whipping into my face. Where was she? Obviously she had decided to continue. The continuation of the walk descended down left along a broad path over a grassy saddle and down to the valley bottom to follow the River Derwent back to Seatoller. Here, you were to follow the river passing Longthwaite Youth Hostel, through Johnny Wood and back to the car park. I looked in both directions and there was no sign of Ann. I decided that she would have completed the route by descending to the river. An hour later I had arrived back at the car park in driving rain. There was no sign of Ann. Then, I knew she had returned by the same route we had taken to Castle Crag. So I set off to retrace the path back to Castle Crag. As I reached the top of the first rise, I could see an approaching group of five people. Moving closer, it was soon obvious that it was Ann with four other people, two elderly couples.

On meeting, it was then that the inquest and recriminations began. Because I had been longer than said, Ann was panicking, fearing I had been blown off the top of Castle Crag. After twenty minutes, the group of four walkers appeared. Explaining her fears, the four walkers tried to help. They lent her their mobile phone and she tried to ring me. Either I couldn't hear it in the rucksack or there was no signal so this was to no avail. One of the party climbed up Castle Crag and returned to say there was no sign of me. Fears of my having fallen off Castle Crag grew. Then they tried to ring Mountain Rescue. Ann did manage to ring both our sons back home. Our eldest son had a friend who was an Air – Sea Rescue helicopter pilot in Stornoway and was set on ringing him. Then the four walkers decided that Ann should walk back to the car park with them. On meeting our sons were rung and the call to Stornoway Air – Sea Rescue was cancelled. Once back at the car we repaid the walkers' favour by ferrying them in the car down to a hotel in Rosthwaite where we all had cream teas with hot mugs of tea or coffee.

---oOo---

A family holiday to Corfu (or Kerkyra in Greek) was blighted with one minor mishap and one major, sad event. Arriving at the sprawling hotel site at the resort of Messongi on the south – east coast with two teenage sons, we were allocated two "chalets" or "cottage rooms". First of all the door to our sons' room was open, the lock was broken and, as they pulled it open it sagged on one hinge. Venturing inside, we found a roughly plastered room with white painted walls, a walk-in shower with filthy plastic curtain and thick, blanket like curtains, akin to a Clint Eastwood poncho which only just clung onto the curtain rail. The bed was next to the living room wall which separated it from the shower. The whole wall was stained with brown patches of damp from shower water seeping through. Two "chalets" away, our room was slightly better but still uninhabitable. Wheeling cases behind, we headed back to the reception in ninety degrees of heat. We found ourselves at the back of queue of people all wishing to change their rooms. An hour later we arrived at the new rooms. They were not exactly "bijou", more basic, but at least clean with no signs of damp and with fully fitted doors which would lock. The holiday had not got off to a very good start.

However, the two boys enjoyed the swimming pool, the basketball and tennis courts and the beautiful, clear and warm waters of the Ionian Sea.

We decided to go on a boat trip to mainland Greece. Dressed in swimming shorts and armed with towels we set sail from Messongi beach. Way out in the Strait of Otrano in the Ionian Sea, we arrived at a huge rock island. A large sea cavern had been carved out from one side. The boat anchored in the mouth of the cave. The water was emerald and clear. We were allowed to jump from the boat and swim in the beautiful waters of the cave. An American lady was saying to friends how she had been scuba diving over at Paleokastritsa on the west coast and brought back sea urchins. As I was about to clamber over the side I stopped to listen in to the rest of the conversation. She said that if you reached your hand to the back of the sea urchin you could scoop them quite easily from their anchorage without any trouble.

With that, I jumped over the side and swam into the cave. My attention was then diverted to the trip leader who was treading water and announcing that if you were a strong enough swimmer you could swim down the water filled tunnel behind him and return by swimming underwater along a submerged tunnel.

Following others I swam down the tunnel and followed it deep into the rock island for a distance of about fifty metres. Reaching a dead end, you had two options. One was to turn and swim back the way you had come. The other was to surface dive and return via the submerged tunnel. Taking a deep breath, I surface-dived and entered the tunnel. Swimming underwater as quickly as I could, I moved along the thirty metre long tunnel eventually surfacing into the open water of the main cave. It was then, as I swam across the cavern, that I remembered the sea urchin story. Down and down I dived in search of sea urchins. At a depth of about twenty feet I could see a cluster of large rocks. Multi-coloured fish darted here everywhere, many different coloured sea anemones waved their little tentacles and there, clinging to the rocks among them was a colony of sea urchins.

Looking up, I could see the bright light shining on the surface above. With puffed cheeks, holding my breath, I reached out towards the back of one of the sea urchins. A sudden, red-hot pain stung the palm of my hand like a thousand sharp needles. Withdrawing my hand, I turned and shot to the surface. Gasping for breath as I surfaced, I swam quickly to the boat. My hand was stinging and throbbing. For the rest of the journey to the Greek mainland, my wife, producing tweezers, pulled out hundreds of black sea urchin needles. After a few days my hand was almost back to normal.

But this was only a minor mishap. The news I was to receive from back home was more serious. A few weeks before we left home, my father had been discharged from hospital and was convalescing at home with stomach cancer. At that time there was only one telephone line out of Messongi. I had decided to ring home to my elder sister to find out how my father was. Finally, after waiting my turn for an hour or so and then spending some time getting a call through, I spoke to my sister. The news was bad. My father was very ill. His condition was terminal and my sister said he might not last very long. Explaining this to our holiday rep, we were allocated to a flight at the end of the first week of our fortnight's holiday. We did arrive home in time and it was two months later that my father actually died.

---oOo---

Celebrating New Year's Eve in Funchal, Madeira, with friends, Lew and Jan, we enjoyed much over indulgence and a magnificent firework display. And so, when the New Year celebration was over we decided that a more dynamic, physical approach was needed. A trip into the interior to trek into the mountains was planned. On previous holidays we had done some levada walking and a comfortable ascent to Madeira's highest peak, Pico Ruivo via Achada do Teixeira. So now, we decided on a circular walk from the village of Fontes. We hired a taxi to take us there and wait for us for the return journey after a three hour walk. This turned out to be less of a mishap or misfortune and more of a danger.

As we clambered into the taxi we should have spotted the potential for hazard when the local taxi driver, in his limited English, declared that he did not know where Fontes was. With maps in hand, acting as Sat Navs, we directed the driver in a westerly direction out of Funchal on the R101. Travelling along the coast we directed him onto the ER229 towards Campanario. On this section of the journey we passed close to the fishing village of Camara de Lobos where Winston Churchill had stayed. He used to paint up on the viewpoint above the harbour, named after him. Just beyond Camara de Lobos was Cabo Girao, the highest coastal cliff in Europe. The cape drops vertically down from the viewing platform. Crossing the Ribeira do Campanario the motorway runs on to Ribeira Brava. Before Ribeira Brava we directed him up a road signposted to Sao Joao and Sao Paulo. Passing a gravel works we drove straight on into Sao Paulo eventually reaching Fontes.

We asked the driver to park in the small village square in front of the Bar Fontes. This was the starting point of the walk. Explaining that it was a three hour walk and indicating the time that we would return, we set off up the tarmac path steeply uphill.

This was lined on either side by a few reed thatched Madeiran cottages. Soon we were on an agricultural path lined with sweet chestnut trees. We pressed on and, after about an hour's ascent, we had a wonderful view into the Ribeira Brava valley. After another seventy five minutes or so, Lewis and I visited the summit of the Chao dos Terreire at a height of 1436 metres. Now we turned downhill back towards Fontes.

Arriving back at the Bar Fontes we were relieved to see the driver sitting in his taxi, fast asleep. Lewis felt sorry for the driver who had hung around for three hours. Rousing the driver, we asked him would he like a drink. Nodding eagerly, he clambered out of the car. Slowly he lumbered over to a bench outside the door of the bar. Quaffing the bottle of beer brought to him, he seemed grateful for the refreshment. But little did we know that we were putting our lives in his hands. Unknown to us, he had spent the afternoon in the Bar Fontes sampling the beers. This was to lead to a never – to – be – forgotten white knuckle ride back to Funchal.

Speeding downhill from Fontes around a switchback of bends, we were thrown from side to side. Lewis was in the front passenger seat and Ann, Jan and I were in the back. Unusually for Lew, he was sitting rigidly, a white pallor to his face. It was then that we realized that the taxi driver was behaving in a somewhat erratic fashion. As we came onto the ER229 again we suspected, as the car lurched across the lanes and back, that the driver was somewhat worse for wear. Jan was tense. Through gritted teeth she snarled at Lewis, 'Do something! Say something to him! We'll all be killed!'

Lewis stared across at the driver. The driver stared ahead in a trance – like state. Lewis went rigid. The three of us in the back trod on imaginary brakes as the taxi careered towards the rear end of a van. At the last moment the driver pulled hard on the steering wheel, swerved out round the van and cut in very close to its front to avoid a collision with the car which was travelling in the opposite direction. There was a blasting of car horn but the taxi was, mercifully, back on its rightful side of the road. This seemed to jolt the driver out of his trance.

Continuing along the ER229, there was now no traffic ahead of us. The driver seemed to settle back into his dream – like state. The taxi veered off every now and then onto the white line in the middle of the road.

'Lewis!' snorted Jan.

Lewis seemed to be in a hypnotic torpor of his own, brought about by pure fear. Jan pushed the back of his seat.

'Lewis, do something!'

Snapping out of his paralysis, Lewis turned to the driver. A horrified look crossed his face as he noticed that the driver's head was jerking forward and backward. His chin would hit his chest and cause him to open his eyes and lift his head up.

'Are you O.K.?' asked Lew, tremulously. 'Do you want to stop?'

The driver just grunted and ignored Lewis. Then we were on the R101, the "motorway" into Funchal.

'Keep talking to him. Keep him awake,' pleaded Jan.

Lewis began an inane banter which suddenly rose to a high pitched crescendo as his squeaking voice blurted, 'Isn't this traffic light on red? It's on stop… it's on stop…'

This did not seem to register with the taxi driver who sped on, bleary – eyed and nodding in his struggle to stay awake.

Now we were all shouting when suddenly the taxi driver braked and we screeched to a halt at the red traffic light. Sitting there, fraught and exhausted, none of us could say anything. Then, with the light still on red, Jan nudged Lewis again. 'Is he asleep? Have a look Lewis! Is he asleep?'

Sure enough, the driver's eyes were closed. His chin was on his chest and he snorted and snored.

'It's green! It's on go!' shouted Lewis, nudging the driver.

Shaking his head and blinking his eyes, the taxi driver looked up. Seeing the green light, he released his hand brake and stamped down on the accelerator. We sped onward and soon, after much swerving, drifting and generally dangerous driving, we arrived, with some relief, on the forecourt of the hotel. We paid the required fare but withheld any tip.

5. Petra, Sinai and The Coloured Canyon

Mishap, misadventure, danger. Ingredients for a memorable holiday. Our trip to Petra, the Sinai and Cairo was one which resulted in real danger.

It was 11.30 p.m. when we arrived at the Queen Alia International Airport in Amman, the capital of Jordan. Meeting up with our travel rep and the other nine travellers on our tour, we sat and waited in the Arrival's Hall for our transport to Petra. It was an hour later when our tour rep led us outside. We boarded a bus which looked like some relic from thirty years ago.

Sitting silently as the bus crawled out of its parking bay, we held our breath, each one probably inwardly thinking: "Will this bus get us to Petra?" Lurching and chugging out of the airport, we set out on the two and a half hour journey along the Desert Highway Route (Highway 15) to the Petra Palace Hotel. Jerking to a halt at the junction to the main highway, empty two litre plastic bottles jumped from beneath the driver's seat and rolled down the aisle. Jumping up, the driver ran down the aisle gathering the bottles frantically and chunnering in Arabic.

Very soon we had left all habitation behind and travelled through the pitch blackness of the desert. About half an hour into the journey we noticed the driver talking in an agitated manner to the tour rep. Then we noticed that there seemed to be condensation or was it steam clouding over the windscreen. The bus slowed and crept along. The road ahead and behind was black and there was no sign of any other vehicle. We were, by now, out in the desert. Not long afterwards the bus came to a stop. Squinting out into the darkness we could see the dark outline of a building. Then the driver grabbed several plastic bottles and left the bus. It was then that our tour rep told us that the delay to our journey was because there had been a problem with the bus. The radiator had been leaking; the engine was overheating causing clouds of steam to travel up the windscreen. We had stopped at a mosque where there was a source of water. The driver returned with full bottles of water and poured them down a gap in the windscreen presumably into the radiator. This was a radiator system I'd never seen before. Time after time he set off, returning with bottles of water which were poured into the radiator. Sometime later he had stored spare full bottles of water around his seat ready for further use.

Realising that we were then travelling through the desert, with little or no habitation, we sat uneasily as the bus rumbled on. It was three o'clock in the morning when we finally reached our hotel in Petra.

Waking the next morning, we had breakfast on the terrace which looked out upon the large smooth boulders and outcrops which were the nursery slopes of the towering, rocky cliffs, the beginning to the sandstone mountains of Petra. The city of Petra was carved from the red sandstone in the 3rd. century B.C. by nomadic tribes known as the Nabateans. It is no wonder that, tucked away in the middle of the desert, the city remained hidden and forgotten for three hundred years after it had been deserted, with only Bedouins living in its caves and tombs. It was rediscovered by the Swiss explorer, Johann Burckhardt in 1812.

Our hotel was just round the corner from the entrance to Petra. So, armed with bottles of water, we set off with our Petra guide, Mohammed, a large Arab in full jaleba and sandals. He had a grey beard and dark, wrinkled skin. Soon, we came to the horse station. Each of us mounted a horse and we were led down by individual horse tenders to the entrance to the main siq where we dismounted. Not for us the Indiana Jones gallop down the siq to the Treasury! The growing numbers of tourists to this unique historical site had posed a Health and Safety risk and an environmental risk to the siq. Two years before my brother had ridden all the way down the siq like a Lancashire Jones hero. On foot we then made our way through the siq - a long, narrow gorge. This channel, eroded by thousands of years of flash floods, forms a twisting, convoluted pathway through the solid rock looming up to 100 metres on either side. Walking leisurely along the siq, marvelling at the differently coloured strata, convinced me that my brother had missed out on a truly magical geological experience.

This siq is about 1.2 kilometers in length and is wide enough for sunlight to pour in, illuminating the dark and gloomy atmosphere. In other places it is only a couple of metres wide and the towering walls appear to close in on you. The wind was whipping and whistling through the gorge and our footsteps echoed metallically.

In the distant past the siq would have been crowded with camel trains, carrying untold objects and items of wealth. The Romans, who later conquered the city in A.D. 106, would have had to fight their way along its entire length.

Rounding the final and narrowest opening of the siq, we were confronted by the towering façade of Al Khazneh, the Treasury, made famous in the film "Indiana Jones and The Last Crusade". As we peered through the gap we were stunned by the Treasury, looking pink and atmospheric as it was bathed in the early morning sunlight. However, we were told the carvings on the Treasury had been damaged by Bedouins who once lived among the ruins, and used them for target practice. On top of the structure is the large urn that the Bedouins shot at in the belief that it contained the lost treasure of King Solomon.

All the great carved frontages, including the Treasury are, in fact, tombs. Exploring the inside of the treasury was disappointing. No huge caverns with tunnels and carved steps leading to the Holy Grail, but a simple cube shaped room with smooth rock walls. But the site of Petra is vast and, although dwellings have long since disappeared, you can still see the seven thousand seat theatre carved out of rock by the Romans and a temple they built when they governed the city.

We followed the main stretch of the ancient Nabotean road which ran past an old market area that would have once been crowded with shoppers and merchants trading goods brought from all over the Middle East. The Bedouin no longer live in the city having been persuaded to move out to a nearby, purpose – built village. They have been given the sole rights to the various tourist concessions on the site. Here, there are a few tables selling ornaments and minerals, nuts and spices.

The heat of the morning was building up. We walked through the site stopping to examine various carved tombs. We climbed the steep steps to the High Place of Sacrifice from where we could see most of the ancient city and the surrounding mountain ridges and summits. From here you can see Mount Hor, known today as Jabal Haroun or Mount Aaron where Moses' brother Aaron is supposedly buried.

On the next day we visited Little Petra – Al Beidha – a site out in the desert where the ancient ruins were older than those at Petra. Disembarking the minibus in the middle of nowhere, we were confronted with rocks and cliffs and siqs choked with the red flowers of the squat oleander trees. We entered through the narrow gorge Siq-al-Barid, meaning the cold siq. In silence we trekked through the dark, eerie canyon. High walls prevented the sunlight penetrating into the siq and, being only a couple of metres wide in parts, it induced a feeling of claustrophobia. The siq opened out into three separate wider areas as we continued on. Emerging at the other end into open spaces, we saw the facades of houses, storage spaces, tombs carved from the sandstone. Moving on, we were headed towards the ruins of a Neolithic village dating back to 7000 B.C. As we went we passed black, goat hair Bedouin tents. Looking inside we could see that the ground was covered with goat hair rugs and cushions. Cooking pots hung over fires. In the distance, on the desert plains, we could just make out the tiny figures of Bedouin tending goats and camels. To one side we passed a couple of tables laden with rocks, trinkets and carved souvenirs. Suddenly a small boy, about five years of age, appeared saying, "You buy? Only one dollar!" Trailing close behind was a girl who looked about two years old. One of the ladies in the group stopped and, feeling sorry for the boy, she presented him with a biscuit. The boy looked at the biscuit, then at the lady, and said: "One for my little sister, too!" The lady gave the girl a biscuit. Walking on, we were soon examining the Neolithic ruins where about sixty houses had been evacuated.

As we returned to the hotel we passed the Bedouin village. This had been purpose-built to relocate the Bedouin from the caves of Petra. What a strange dichotomy! Newly built houses lined the streets which were merely dirt tracks. The houses were simple one storey square blocks, whitewashed, with small windows and flat roofs. But on the roofs or in their "back gardens" were large satellite dishes. Cars parked on the dirt track outside the houses were interspersed with camels tied up on Wild West styled, wooden horse rails. Goats roamed and foraged along the dirt track.

---oOo---

From Petra we travelled down to Aquaba to take the ferry across the Gulf of Aquaba to Nuweiba City on the Sinai Peninsula. Arriving at the ferry terminal we crawled into a queue. Well, it wasn't so much a queue as a morass of cars, vans and buses sprawled across the waiting area. There seemed no order to this ferry embarkment. What immediately became obvious was the number of cars overloaded with "white goods". Cars and vans were covered with a film of sand and dust. Many had large dents and rusted holes in the body work. An estate car just in front of us was laden on a makeshift roof rack with a fridge, a cooker, and stacks of bedding and boxes. Suddenly there was a startling explosion. The rear window of the estate car had collapsed under the load and glass shattered and flew everywhere. The driver, already outside his car, smoking, calmly walked to the back of the car, and checked that his load was still secure then returned to his passengers chatting as if nothing had happened. Our tour guide told us that many of the people in the cars and vans were Egyptians who worked in Saudi Arabia and when they were returning home loaded their vehicles with the "white goods" which were cheaper and were available.

Gradually we inched our way towards the ferry. Once aboard the ferry we headed south down the gulf to Nuweiba. Once there we passed through what can only be described as a series of warehouses which was customs. Emerging at the other side we were in Sinai, part of Egypt. We travelled on around the gulf coast until we reached a hotel complex on the outskirts of Nuweiba City. We were to stay here for a couple of days before moving on down Sinai to St. Catherine's Monastery and then following the coast northwards towards the Suez Tunnel and Cairo.

The following day a jeep safari trip had been organized to visit the Coloured Canyon out in the desert. We set off in two four – wheeled drive vehicles along a smooth, well surfaced highway. By a cluster of date palms we turned off onto a gravel road which then ran into the off-road trek across the Wadi Watir. We trundled and buffeted across the desert, edged in the distance by the limestone mountain chain El Tih where, it is said, Moses was lost for forty years. Apart from rock and sand the only vegetation was lonely acacias and tamarisk trees.

Finally we arrived at the edge of a huge "hole" in the desert. Ten metres from the jeeps, steep slopes fell into the Coloured Canyon which was scarred with many rock foundations. Looking over the edge, I joked that at least we wouldn't have to descend by that route. Hearing what I had said, our young Egyptian guide said, "Yes, this is the way we go down." Our guide was in his early thirties, wearing glasses and dressed quite casually in jeans and polo shirt. By now the temperature had risen to the high eighties. Our entire group, apart from the guide, wore a hat. On bottoms and digging heels into the loose sandstone we descended in "scree walking" style down the slope into the canyon. Once on the wide floor of the canyon we set off towards the labyrinths of rocky formations.

Soon we entered a maze of narrow slot canyons which twisted and turned in every direction. The cliff walls of these siqs towered eighty metres above us. Layers of minerals in the sandstone formed amazing, beautiful swathes of colour – pinks, purples, silver and gold. In single file we picked our way along the narrow chasms, in some parts only a metre in width. It could only be described as upright pot – holing! We had to clamber over large boulders and rock climb over others. Then we had to descend smooth rock slides and push our way through rock tunnels drilled and carved by past water erosion. As we continued the temperatures had soared to nearly one hundred degrees Fahrenheit.

Sometime later we emerged from the meandering siqs into bright, hot sunlight. We were in a wide, flat clearing surrounded by craggy, sandstone cliffs. Sheltering in the shade of an overhang, sipping from our bottles of water, our guide then told us that this was only the second time he had led this trip and that he wasn't sure where the Bedouin tent was – our finishing point. Asking us to wait in the shade, he set off up a winding path to get up onto the flat tops of the cliffs in order to see where the Bedouin refuge lay. Walking along the top, he shaded his eyes to scan the distance. Then he stopped and pointed ahead, shouting down to us that he could see the encampment and that was the direction in which we were going to trek. It was then that the problems began. Suddenly he strode to the edge of the cliff. Sitting down, he dangled his legs over the edge into a narrow cleft which travelled down the height of the rock face. Everyone watched in silence wondering what on earth he was doing. Swivelling round to face the rock, his right foot reached down to jam itself onto a small ledge.

'Look! I think he's going to climb down,' said Derek, one of our group.

Indeed he began to gain hand holes and inch slowly down the cleft. Instead of returning by the safe path by which he had ascended, he was now rock climbing down the twenty foot rock face. This face ended on a flat platform which fell down another eight feet or so onto the canyon floor. Halfway down loose rocks beneath his feet bounced down onto the platform. With fingernail grip he became motionless. A minute passed by and he didn't move; he couldn't move.

'Bloody Hell!' said Norman, one of our elderly fellow travellers, 'I think he's stuck.'

'Had we better try to help him?' someone said.

Sweat was running down my neck in the searing heat. It seemed that nobody dare move. Then more rock seemed to crumble beneath his feet and tumble down onto the rocks below. Before another word could be uttered, the guide loosened his grip and fell backwards from the rock face. Everyone watched in disbelief as he fell, landing flat on his back onto the platform, then bouncing over the edge to the canyon floor below. His glasses had flown off and he lay still on his back.

'God, he's fallen!' said Norman.

'He must be badly hurt…' began one of the ladies.

'Is he… is he dead?' asked another.

'Come on,' said Derek. 'We'd better go and see to him. Ladies, stay here out of the sun.'

Derek, me and a younger male member, Karl, picked our way over rubble and boulders to reach where the guide lay.

The guide lay motionless, flat on his back. Moving his head from side to side, he groaned. He was alive. But he had come to rest with jagged rocks on either side of his head. Had his head struck one of these he would surely be dead. Struggling to move, he winced in pain.

'Don't try to move. Just lie still,' said Derek. 'We don't know what you may have damaged.'

'Have you got a mobile phone?' I said. 'We can contact someone to help. Is there a helicopter rescue service we can contact?'

'No…no…' mumbled the guide. 'Phones no signal out here… no rescue…none round here…nearest…hospital…many miles…Cairo…' Then he tried to push himself up on his elbows.

'No, don't try to move. Lie still, we'll get you a drink of water.'

The guide hadn't even brought a bottle of water with him. It was now midday and the heat was unbearable. We realised that, trapped in this strange environment, miles from anywhere, in this heat, would be dangerous. We knew we had to get him to safety. Karl went back to the others for a bottle of water. Derek crouched over the guide to make sure he lay still. I scoured the area for his glasses but they were nowhere to be seen.

'I'll have to…stay put…for…a short time,' gasped the guide. 'The Bedouin…Bedouin tent…in that direction. You go. Further on there is…another group. You'll come to them. Go… go to the tent with them. They'll…get help…'

Karl went back to the others to lead them to the other group and then to the final destination. Derek and I were to stay with the guide until he felt well enough to move.

As the group disappeared across the open space and threaded their way into the narrow entrance of the labyrinth, Derek and I crouched over the fallen guide.

We gave him a drink of water and he seemed to recover a little. First aid tells you not to move someone in this situation until the expert help of paramedics has arrived. But there wouldn't be any ambulance or paramedic or expert help down there in the middle of the Sinai Desert at the bottom of the Coloured Canyon. We knew that somehow we had to get him out of this heat and back to safety. After a few minutes we supported him as he insisted that he sat up. He was reassuring us that he was only winded and that, if we gave him five minutes, he would be able to get to his feet.

Wincing with pain, we helped him to his feet, supporting him with his arms round each of our shoulders and our arms around his back. Stumbling a few metres forward, we stopped as he wheezed and breathed heavily. As we edged forward towards the narrow, twisting siqs, we anticipated the difficulties that the obstacles would present.

As we shuffled and manoeuvred along the first narrow chasms, up ahead our group had met the other party. This party was made up of 18 – 30's, mainly bikini clad Italian girls. Ogling over these nubile, young ladies, their guides were not interested in the plight of our mainly geriatric party. They merely pointed out the route to the Bedouin tents up on the far edge of the canyon, and continued on their way.

Progress along the siq was slow. Every few metres we had to stop. When the siq became very narrow we had to turn sideways and move along in a crab – like manner. Soon we came to a large rock fall. I quickly scrambled to the top of the rock whilst Derek supported the guide. Lying on top of the rock, I reached down. As Derek pushed him up from below I gripped him under both armpits and pulled him up. Gradually we pulled and pushed. The guide cried out in pain. But we managed to get him to the top of the rock and lay him on his back. Derek climbed up onto the rock; I slid down the other side of the rock. I supported the guide's feet and Derek held his arms as we slid him down the rock. Following him, Derek jumped down and we, once again, supported him. Slowly we struggled along the siq, managing the many obstacles.

Meanwhile the rest of our group had emerged from the labyrinth of slot canyons into the wide, open arena of the canyon floor. Above the end of the canyon, perched on top of cliff edges, were the Bedouin tents. Standing motionless, they scanned the sandstone bluffs looking for a way up to the encampment.

'Over there,' said Karl suddenly, pointing as he moved forward. 'There's a path winding up to the top.'

It was with no great confidence and with some trepidation that the group strode across the canyon to a fairly indistinct path etched out of the sandstone cliff. The path was about two to three feet wide and wound its way upwards clinging to the rock face. Gingerly, each of the party stepped onto the path and, in single file started on the ascent.

Slowly but surely, we manoeuvred the injured guide through the siqs. Every so often we stopped to give him a rest and a drink. Sliding around the next bend, we came face to face with our greatest challenge. The siq was blocked by a large rock face. It would have been a dead end but for a hole drilled through it. The hole sloped downwards and at its bottom end it led out to the floor of the siq with a five foot drop. Going feet first, you had to insert yourself into the hole and then, as if in a tube slide at some water park, you slid down and then dropped the last five feet into the siq. Making a chair with our joined hands, we lifted the guide and placed his legs into the hole. Derek held his head and shoulders whilst I scrambled up the rock face, over the top of it and clambered down to where the hole emerged into the siq. Then I thrust my head and shoulders into the hole. Derek lowered the guide into the hole. I stopped his feet as he slid down and held him there. Slowly I let him slide until his feet and legs emerged from the hole. Supporting his legs, I guided them down until his feet stood on the rocky floor and then held him up against the rock. Derek slid down and out of the hole. Together we once again supported the guide, and continued our journey through the siqs. After the hole in the rock the rest of the route through the siqs was manageable.

Reaching the safety of the Bedouin tents, our group dashed over to the Bedouin guides and told them what had happened. Their first reaction was to laugh uncontrollably. Their second reaction was to shrug their shoulders and settle back down onto their cushions, unmoved and unbothered. After further pleas for assistance, two Bedouins set off with a blanket on which they were to carry the injured guide. By this time we had reached the path and half way along met the two Bedouin. Our guide refused any help and insisted that he was O.K. and that, with our support, could get to the top without the aid of a Bedouin blanket.

On the way back to our hotel our guide was in considerable discomfort as the jeep jolted and juddered across the Wadi Watir. Once back, the guide gave us the meeting time for the following morning's journey onward to St. Catherine's Monastery then up the western route of the Sinai to Cairo. He assured us that he would be visiting his local hospital in Cairo. Limping away, he headed for his room, not to be seen again until the following morning.

The next morning we set off in our mini – coach southwards towards Mount Sinai and St. Catherine's Monastery. Our guide sat uncomfortably with a cushion behind him, saying very little during the journey. St. Catherine's Monastery nestled at the foot of the great rock base of Mount Sinai. Great, smooth rounded rocks rose above the Monastery to the summit of Mount Sinai some 7497 feet in height. We looked up, in awe, at the great rock mountain where Moses had supposedly received the rock tablets inscribed with the Ten Commandments. In times past the only way into the monastery was to be hauled up in a large basket. Now, conveniently, there were large entrance gates. Photographs were taken inside the Monastery in front of a small bushy shrub – like tree reputedly said to be "The Burning Bush". We were told that this shrub was unique and was only to be found in the Monastery. Many people had taken away cuttings and tried to propagate them elsewhere but with no success.

Our guide slept for the rest of the journey up the west coast of the Sinai Peninsula towards Suez, the tunnel and onwards to Cairo and the Pyramids.

We had seen many wonderful sights on this trip but what will always be long – remembered is our real adventure in the Coloured Canyon.

6. Bats, Fireflies and Other Natural Phenomena

It is sometimes the unusual or the unexpected which enrich holiday experiences. Planned trips on which everything proceeds like clockwork are often forgettable. But when some magical moment suddenly takes you unaware, then it remains long in the memory.

Having toured Northern France, visiting Mont St. Michel, the Bayeux Tapestry and St. Malo, my wife and I drove down to a gite not far from Saumur, near the Loire. We were to join friends, Lewis and Jan, who had already spent a week there. Arriving late in the afternoon we settled in and ate al fresco. Hot weather had followed us from the north and the temperature was thirty degrees. The atmosphere was very oppressive.

Enjoying chilled wine and several games of cards, we all decided to call it a night. As we cleared up, ready to go up to the bedrooms, Lewis said, 'Oh, a word of warning. Don't be tempted to open your windows very wide. In fact I'd keep the wooden shutters closed. Last night we had the window fully opened and we had a visitor – a bat!'

'Yes,' said Jan, 'and Lewis hid under the duvet as it flew around. We closed the bedroom door and eventually it found its way out.'

'They're roosting in that ruined granary building along the track where you drove in.'

Taking the advice seriously, we set the window on its stay so that there was only a narrow opening and closed the shutters leaving another narrow opening. However, it was very hot in the room and there was little air. After about half an hour we were both sweltering and gasping for air. Not long after we decided that we had to open the shutters and window wider – bats or no bats!

Draughts of cooler air came as a welcome relief and we began to doze and drop off to sleep. I don't know how long I'd been asleep when I was suddenly awakened by a series of nudges.

'Listen. What's that?' my wife whispered heavily.

'What? What's what?'

'That noise. Like …flapping…'

It was pitch black in the room. Then, sure enough, I could hear this continually drumming, droning sound. It whirred above our heads and headed back cross the room.

'It's a bat! It must be…'

I flicked on the bedside light. Sure enough a bat was flitting back and forth across the room.

'Do something! Get rid of it!'

Then the bat settled and hung upside down on a beam above our bed.

'Get rid of it!' screeched my wife. She jumped out of bed, dashed through the door and shut it firmly, leaving me locked in the room with the bat.

The commotion had awakened Lew and Jan. The three of them stood on the landing urging me to chase the bat out of the bedroom. Standing up on the bed, I waved a pillow towards the roosting bat, shouting, 'Shoo! Go on, get out of here!'

Taking flight again, the bat fluttered across the room and back, almost dive – bombing me. Back and forth it went in a frenzy. Quickly I ran over to the window and opened both it and the shutters as wide as possible. Waving my arms wildly, I chased the bat back and forth across the room but to no avail. It was then that I adopted my toreador stance. With duvet in front of me, I flapped it about like a bullfighter's cape. Stepping as if dancing the paso doble, I moved across the room. Jumping onto the bed, I raised the duvet, obstructing the bat's flight. Swerving it careered back towards the window. Before it could fully return I moved forward with my "duvet-cape", shouting, 'Torro! Torro! Out you go!'

Finally the bat wheeled and found the opening of the window. Feverishly, I dashed over and closed both windows and shutters. After that we left both window and shutters slightly opened and settled down once again. To this day, my role as "bat fighting toreador" had not been forgotten.

---oOo---

Another, earlier trip to France left us with another memorable moment. My father had often told me stories about my grandfather who had been killed in the First World War. The family myth was that he had been killed on Armistice Day, 11th. November, 1918. He told us that grandfather had been a coal miner and did not need to enlist in the army. Having to walk to the pit, a distance of six miles, and toil in dirty and difficult conditions, he decided that "going to war" would be a great adventure. Enlisting in the Lancashire Fusiliers, 19th. Battalion in 1914, he went to training camps and then tours of duty. No one in the family knew where he had fallen and where he was buried – only that it was somewhere in Northern France. We promised my father that we would find out where he had fought and where he was buried.

Accessing the War Graves Commission website on line, we discovered my grandfather's war records. We learnt that he was indeed in the Lancashire Fusiliers, 19th. Battalion and that he had been killed near the small settlement of Haspres Coppice, halfway between Cambrai and Valenciennes on the France-Belgium border. We also discovered that he had been killed on 13th. October, 1918, but not on Armistice Day. As, in that campaign, one of the Pioneer Corps digging the trenches, he was not involved in active fighting. However, in early October, 1918, orders were issued for a "big push" to drive the Germans over the River Sel and backwards into Belgium. So fierce was the battle that all able-bodied men were to take up arms and charge in ranks. On October 13th, joining in such a surge, my grandfather was hit by a sniper's bullet from the retreating Germans. Fifteen men from 19th. Battalion were felled on that day and buried nearby in a small plot which was to become a cemetery tended to by local Frenchmen.

We discovered all this in April 1990 just at the same time that my father fell ill and was hospitalised with stomach cancer. Telling him all the details, we promised that when he was feeling better we would take him to visit the grave. However, his illness became progressively worse and by September of 1990 he had died. This made us very determined to travel to France and find my grandfather's resting place.

In the following year we planned a holiday to the South of France, with a stopover near Cambrai with the sole intention of finding Hapres Coppice.

Using maps, the three of us – my wife, Ann, youngest son Stuart and I – drove out of Cambrai on our quest. There was one signpost to Hapres and then, nothing else. Empty country roads wound in every direction. Somewhere we must have taken a wrong turning. We travelled through the countryside, past fields and copses and woods through a landscape devoid of human habitation. Everywhere looked the same as we seemed to be travelling around in circles. We were lost. Reaching a junction, Ann said, 'Go this way. I don't know why but something is telling me that it's just down here. It's like something or someone is guiding us.' This road looked the same as all the others and I was doubtful. Then, Stuart told me to slow down. As I did so, on our left, we saw white, marble steps and a white cross. We stopped. Crossing the road, we began to walk up the steps.

'Look,' said Ann. 'Down there.'

Along the edge of the road was a grassy ditch and, just by the steps in the ditch, were three red poppies. We climbed the steps and there, in front of us, was a row of white, marble headstones. The cemetery was quite narrow and about as long as a medium sized lawn. There were 64 headstones. Walking along in silence we reached Headstone Number 62 – my grandfather's grave. The grass was beautifully mown and the narrow flower bed all the way along was immaculate, neatly tended without a weed in sight. We stood and viewed the landscape. There were fields and woods but not a building in sight. Looking across to the nearest woodland, I wondered if that was where the battalion was heading and if that was where the fatal shot had come from. In these moments, from taking the road at the junction to standing in front of my grandfather's headstone, we all felt that my father had been with us and guided us there. We had fulfilled our promise; we had taken him to his father's grave.

Solemnly we laid a small poppy wreath that we had brought against the headstone. In a small wall at the top of the steps we opened a metal door. Inside was a book. It listed all those buried there. We found my grandfather's name, army number and date of death. Buried there also were those who had fallen in a second surge on October 20th. 1918. As we left the small plot, Ann gathered the three poppies growing in the ditch. The next day we travelled on down to the South of France where we enjoyed a relaxing stay.

Later, when we had returned home, we went to visit the only surviving child of my grandfather, my father's sister, Aunt Edith. She was, by now, ninety years old. She cried when she saw the photographs of her father's grave. We gave her a small album of photographs with a pressed poppy in the front. It was then that I enquired about the family myth that grandfather had been killed on Armistice Day when really he had been killed on 13th. October, 1918.

Aunt Edith explained:

'I remember it as if it was yesterday. I was seven years old. It was 11th. November – Armistice Day. I went to answer a knock on the door. A man gave me a telegram. It was a telegram to tell us that father had been killed in action on October 13th.'

---oOo---

Unexpected natural phenomena also remain long in the memory. One such occurrence was on a family holiday to Lake Bled (now in Slovenia) which was a resort in the old Yugoslavia at that time. We were on holiday with Mike and Margaret's family in pre "Underpants" days. There were our two sons, Steven and Stuart and Mike and Margaret's boys, Liam and David. One evening we went for dinner to a small restaurant on Bled Island. It was a lovely, warm evening with a clear sky. Aboard a pletna, a traditional wooden boat, propelled by a gondola-like oarsman with two large bladed oars, we set off for the island. The sun was dipping between the gaps in the surrounding Julian Alps creating a perfect backdrop to the placid, green water of the lake. Thirty minutes later we arrived at the docking steps on the island.

Bled Island is not very large and its main building is the pilgrimage church of The Assumption of Mary.

We ascended the steps and entered the old castle like building in which the restaurant was located.

Having enjoyed a delicious meal, we began the return journey. The oars of the pletna dipped into the water rhythmically, the quiet lapping creating a soporific mood. Halfway across the lake, under a black, star studded sky, we relaxed in the warm, late evening atmosphere. These moments seemed serene and magical. Suddenly there were cries from Steven, Stuart, Liam and David: 'Look! Up there! Look!' Everyone looked up at the black, night sky. There, scoring across the blackness above, a shooting star grabbed our attention. This was the beginning of a light show which would outshine any firework display or laser show. Countless shooting stars traced across the darkness. Everyone lay back in awed silence and witnessed this spectacle which lasted for the whole thirty minute journey back to shore. This was an unexpected, magical moment which will never be forgotten.

---oOo---

Another family holiday took us to Tuscany. Having left Pisa airport, we drove to a small bed and breakfast hotel, Poggio Leo, near San Gimione where we stayed overnight before travelling on the next day to our holiday farmhouse. Just behind Poggio Leo was a larger hotel with a restaurant. So Ann and I, along with Steven and his wife Natascha and Stuart and his wife Anne-Marie, walked through the small garden across a track to the restaurant. We dined on an outside terrace overlooking the beautiful Tuscan landscape. Eating a typical rustic meal of wild boar or duck washed down by a local, red wine, we relaxed under the infinite Tuscan sky. It was on the short journey back to our bed and breakfast lodgings that an unexpected surprise awaited us. In the pitch black we opened the gate to the garden. In front of us the dark flowers and shrubs were aglow, twinkling and shimmering with thousands of tiny spots of light. We were rooted to the spot and stayed put for many minutes hypnotized by the clouds of fireflies which flittered and glowed all over the garden.

When we departed the next morning we thought that we were leaving behind the unexpected. The unexpected, though, happened again. But this was not a natural occurrence but human error. Having packed the Espace, the tailgate boot was closed. Or so we thought! Everyone clambered in. My eldest son was the driver. Because of my driving habits when abroad

– mainly signalling opposite to the direction in which we were travelling (turning left I described it as "right as I know it") – I was consigned to a cramped seat in the boot clinging onto the cases. Turning onto the main road we began to drive uphill. It was then that it was revealed that the tailgate boot was not closed properly. As we accelerated up the slope, the tailgate flew open. I grabbed in vain as cases flew out then clung onto the seat with a strangled shout as I began to be ejected as well. My son pulled to a sudden halt. Cases and bags were deposited in a neat line on the road behind us. I managed not to join them. Fifty yards behind us was a tourist coach. Having seen the incident, the coach driver had slowed down and then stopped. He jumped out, ran up the road and helped us to gather the cases and pack them back in the

Espace. We moved on with the tailgate firmly shut.

Our Tuscan holiday began in a memorable fashion.

7. Unusual Occurrences

On a trip to China we arrived to the sort of great acclaim reserved for celebrities. Our group of five was the first touring party after the Sars epidemic. It was July 2003. Visits were made to the usual tourist spots. In Beijing we visited the Forbidden City, Tiananmen Square, a local Hutong dwelling and a trip to the Great Wall of China. Here Chinese tourists were fascinated by our small group and we spent our time posing with them for photo shoots. Asking one group why they were so keen on having their photograph with us, the answer was, 'You, Big Noses. Very good. Big Noses.'

We also travelled to Nanjing and Wutan and of course the "must – see" spectacle of the Terracotta

Warriors in Xian. This is a truly wonderful excavation and was one of the main highlights of the tour.

Another highlight was a three day cruise on the Yangste River through the Three Gorges of Qutang, Wu and Xiling. As we travelled upstream we were soon sailing between towering gorge sides. The construction of the Three Gorges Dam was resulting in the rising of the river level thus reducing the dramatic height of the gorge sides. However, still under construction, water levels had not yet risen very much and the gorge was both dramatic and domineering.

Cruising through the brown waters of the Xiling Gorge, we were transfixed by the towering cliffs on either side. White limestone, green vegetation, clusters of trees clinging from every possible cleft and crag lined the sides of the gorge.

On reaching the Three Gorges Dam, still under construction, we were impressed by its immensity. It was here that we had to be raised up to the river level over 300 feet above if we were to continue our journey. Travelling up through the staircase of the five ship locks, it took us two to three hours.

Continuing on our cruise, everything was serene and beautiful. We were running against the flow of the river when, suddenly, someone spotted an object in midstream. It was moving quickly with the current. As it passed us we then realized that it was, in fact, a body. A man's body, face down in the water, swept by us. Alarmed, a number of our party reported the sighting to our tour guide so that he could inform the captain of the boat. The tour guide told us not to worry; that the captain would have seen the body; that it was a common occurrence; and that he'd probably committed suicide or fallen in upstream working on the river.

After this, the journey continued without further incident. The following day we cruised onwards, reaching at midday, at the Eastern mouth of the Wu Gorge, an inlet where the river widened. Taking a smaller ferry boat from our tour boat we headed to the inlet. Here was a curved bay where we moored at a dockside. There were a few buildings clinging to the edge of the bay – a shop and a restaurant. And moored all along the harbour was a flotilla of long, wooden boats. They were flat sampans which the locals called "Peapod" boats. The Shennong Stream flowed from the mountains into the opposite side of the bay. The stream rises in the forests of the

Shennongjia Natural Protectorate and is about 60 kilometres in length. The "Peapod" style rafts were used to navigate the fast flowing and sometimes narrow and shallow waters of the Shennong Stream. Each "Peapod" raft could hold about 12 passengers and was manned by six boatmen. Four of these were "trackers". As our party boarded the "Peapods" and clad ourselves in yellow life jackets, the four "trackers" sat on the bow. These boatmen are Tuja and were well used to navigating up and down the Shennong. Rowers on either side of the boat and a helmsman stood up and we set off across the bay towards the Shennong.

The gorge through which the Shennong flowed was stunningly beautiful. Wavelets of emerald green water buffeted against the boat as we moved upstream against the current. Towering peaks of limestone cliffs loomed over us on either side. The white limestone, the different hues of green from trees and shrubs which crowded and clung to sides of the gorge melded with the blue sky and the emerald green water. The wooden oars dipped silently into the water as we entered narrow chasms. The now obsidian water added to the mood of beauty, tranquility and calmness. Then the gorge widened again and the sunlight lit everything a golden green. As we went the guide pointed out caves in the limestone cliffs and stalactites hanging on both sides of the bank. "Plank roads" clung to the base of the gorge just above the water level. These enabled fishermen to access the water and moor their boats. In the recesses in the cliff sides were the old burial sites of the Bai people. Here, the "hanging coffins" had been set up more than a thousand years ago.

But soon we could see the river course was choked with boulders, large pebbles and cusped pebble beaches. The stream struggled over this deposition and the water became very shallow. Suddenly the rowers drew in their paddles and we came to a halt. Then the four "trackers" jumped out into the water, clad only in shorts. Ropes made from braided bamboo strips were unravelled from the hull of the boat and thrown into the water. The "trackers" grabbed the ropes which had white cloth slings knotted into them at intervals. With the slings across one shoulder, the "trackers" struggled along the stream bed pulling the boat over the rocks and through the shallow water. With great effort, bent double, with both hands and feet pushing against the stream bed, the "trackers" slowly and gradually pulled the boat through the shallows. Eventually, reaching the deeper pool of water upstream, the "Peapod" was once again afloat. Ropes were coiled again and thrown back into the boat. The four "trackers" stood at either side of the boat, now in thigh deep water, pushing the boat ahead until the rowers could dip their oars in again. Standing in the water, holding the boat's side, the "tracker" grinned at us and lifted a knotted plastic bag out of the water. Unknotting the bag, he took something out and said cheerily, 'You want to buy postcards. Only one dollar for all.' With that he opened up the concertina package containing eight postcards. Impressed by such enterprise, how could we not outlay one dollar to secure a souvenir of this memorable trip?

The cover of the postcard showed us how this had been done in the past, as earlier told to us by our guide. The "trackers" used to ply their trade completely naked. Many of the ladies on our "Peapod" were rather disappointed.

Our journey upstream continued. As we went we spotted macaque monkeys trampling in the trees which now clung in dense clusters to the edges of the gorge. Soon, however, the rowers slowed, and then began back paddling until we were facing downstream. Having been told to keep limbs safely inside the boat, the oarsmen skulled forward, drew in the oars, and let the current take the boat. Down the stream we charged in an exhilarating "white knuckle" ride.

Back at the landing stage, we were ferried back to our tour boat and continued on our journey through the Xiling Gorge.

---oOo---

Unable to land in the U.S.A. at Chicago O'Hare airport because of tremendous thunderstorms which had flooded the runways, we were diverted 220 miles southwards to Indianapolis. Not now having enough fuel to return to Chicago, we spent three hours in an aircraft queue waiting to refuel. To be told that the closure of O'Hare was not an unusual occurrence at this time of the year, did nothing to quell impatience, boredom, frustration and anger. Nearly every flight into O'Hare had been diverted to Indianapolis. Having refuelled, we now joined the runway traffic jam to await our turn for takeoff. Once in the air it didn't take us long to fathom that there would be little time left to check in onto our connecting flight to Las Vegas. Finally landing at O'Hare at Terminal 1 we had ten to fifteen minutes to check in for our flight.

The problem was that the Las Vegas flight departed from Terminal 4.

Dashing onto a shuttle train, we arrived at check-in. An official told us to quickly put our luggage onto a conveyor belt. Then we went to check-in only to be told that the flight was closed. We were checked in onto the next flight, on the following morning at 9.30 and given vouchers to stay at the Chicago Hilton overnight.

'Just get the Hilton Shuttle Bus outside,' we were told. It was now midnight and stepping outside we were met with chaos. Hundreds of people were waiting to get on different Shuttle Buses to different hotels. Eventually we arrived at the hotel at 1 a.m.

This was not a good start to our American Adventure and the next morning brought us, or should I say me, further discomfort. Armed with luggage my wife spotted the airport transfer bus as it pulled up outside. Having just sent me to the desk to enquire about the time of the next shuttle, she now called out across the entrance foyer to hurry as a bus had arrived. Rushing headlong to negotiate the revolving glass doors, I decided it would be quicker to go through one of the passages at either side. What I thought was an exit was, in fact, a reinforced glass panel. There were no stickers or other markings on these panels to indicate that they were, actually, glass. Leaping forward, I crashed into the glass, nose first. Sharp pain was followed by blood gushing from my nose and smearing across my face. Not seeing what had happened, Ann, my wife, came back through the revolving doors to announce, 'It's O.K. That's not ours. It's already full. The next one's…'

Seeing the blood pumping from my nostrils, she said, 'Oh, here you'd better have a tissue. And you'll need a plaster on that. Better go to the desk and ask for one.'

With blooded nose and soggy, red tissue, I stood in front of the desk.

'Yes, sir, what can I do for you?' asked the very unobservant desk clerk.

'Er, id's my dose. Have you got a plaster, please?'

'Sorry, sir, we don't have anything by that name.'

'For the blood. A plaster.'

'Sorry, I don't understand, sir.'

With a sudden brainwave, my wife stepped forward. 'A Band-Aid. He needs a Band-Aid for his nose.'

After this translation from English into Pseudo-English, we were furnished with plasters. The bleeding was staunched and the plaster applied. We boarded the bus to the airport, checked in and, soon, at last, were on our way to Las Vegas.

On reaching Las Vegas airport, having enquired at a baggage desk, we were directed to the centre of the huge Arrivals Hall. People were milling about everywhere and there, amongst a pile of about one hundred, unsupervised, unmarked bags and cases, we found our luggage. Not quite the top security we had imagined! From there we set off to "Treasure Island", our themed Las Vegas hotel on the Strip for the next four days. Our taxi driver to "Treasure Island" nonchalantly announced, 'Gone a lot cooler today. Down to 100 degrees. Yesterday it was 130.'

Staying in the "Treasure Island" hotel we were privileged to witness the four times nightly sinking of the English navy ship at the hands of the Pirate ship. Knowing that friends Colin and Jean were also heading for Las Vegas and then to Yosemite and Mammoth Lakes we had arranged to meet them at our hotel the next day. We dined together and Colin advised us that any trip up to Death Valley by car would need two, two gallon bottles of water. The next day we both took separate trips by air to the Grand Canyon. We went on an eight seater light aircraft, they went by helicopter. Later, when we met up at Yosemite they told us about their eventful flight. The pilot claimed to have flown helicopters in Vietnam and demonstrated all the skills that he had learned such as descending rapidly between crags and then swooping upwards to skim the tops of towering cliffs. It was only when we returned home that we learned of an horrific crash by an helicopter carrying eight tourists to the Grand Canyon. All eight plus the pilot were killed. The description of the ex -Vietnam pilot and his antics matched that of the pilot who had flown our friends.

---oOo---

Four days later, after visiting an indoor Venice complete with canals and gondolas inside the Venetian Hotel, the constant erupting of a volcano at the Mirage, Tutankhamen's tomb at the Luxor, the Roman forum at Caesar's Palace, the fountains at the Bellagio dancing to the highs and lows of the singing voices of Sarah Brightman and Andrea Bocelli telling us it was "Time to say goodbye" and a light aircraft trip over the Grand Canyon, we arrived back at Las Vegas airport.

Here, we were to pick up our hire car and set out on our Great American Adventure. Our self - drive tour was to take us onward to Death Valley, then around the southern end of the Rockies, into the San Joaquin or Central Valley of California, up to Yosemite National Park and finishing at San Francisco.

At the airport we collected a silver Buick. We did not get off to a good start when I was unable to move the driver's seat to take up a comfortable driving position. This was the first of my minor embarrassments as I called over the hire car attendant. I should have known that the seat moved electronically. After all we were in the U.S.A.! Having started the car, I was feeling fully in charge. But then I couldn't find the gear stick. Cleverly, I realised it was an automatic and I needed to put it into "drive mode". After several minutes of confusion and the uttering of various expletives, I had to call the attendant back. Why did I not know that you had to press the brake pedal to put it into "Drive"? What could be more logical? Now we were ready for the Great American Journey. Pressing the accelerator we lurched forward, shuddered and came to a halt. Sensing that he would be needed again, the attendant was still at the side of the car observing progress – or should I say, the lack of it!

With a hand raised, he bent forward to inform me that I had to take off the hand brake. Of course! But I had looked for any sign of a hand brake and there was none. Thus, stupidly, I assumed this would be part of the automatic system of the car. Looking confused and shaking my head, I was given the last piece of information that I needed to drive out of Las Vegas airport. The hand brake was down below the dashboard just above my left foot. The hand brake was, in fact, a foot brake. Once again American logic reared its ugly head. Now why didn't I think of that? Now, in complete charge, we drove slowly towards the airport exit. Looking through my rear view mirror, I could see the attendant just standing there, shaking his head. I doubt he could see me driving away, shaking my head!

  Driving northwards, we followed our map looking for Interstate 95. There were numerous routes signposted for Cedar Road, Oak Street, Beech Avenue but no obvious signpost for that less important route – Interstate 95! And so, for the next hour, we ended up driving around the outskirts of Las Vegas. It was by sheer chance that, coming round again past familiar landmarks, we slowed down at a fork in the road, and there, painted in white on the road to the left was the symbol of our salvation – I-95. There was no sign of a signpost.

At last we were on our way from Las Vegas on the Interstate 95, heading for Amargosa Valley. But our advice from Colin about Death Valley warned us that it would be wise to carry extra water in case of an overheated engine. Thus, we stopped at the first, and probably only, gas station on the route to buy two, two gallon bottles of water. And so we continued.

After a while, as we were going up a hill, my wife, Ann, began one of her numerous panics.

'Look! Look at the engine temperature! It's rising and rising. We'll have to stop!'

Turning the air conditioning off, we observed the temperature dropping again. But in the intense heat we were both dripping with sweat and gasping in the hot, airless car. Immediately I opened the window. It was like a blast from a furnace. The heat smacked us in the face. As quickly as possible, I closed the window. So we drove on suffering from this discomfort but safe in the knowledge that the temperature gauge was back to normal.

Reaching the Amargosa Valley junction, we turned off left down Highway 373. Then, at Death Valley Junction, we turned right along Highway 190 en route to Furnace Creek Ranch, the destination for our first overnight stay.

Four miles from Furnace Creek ranch we stopped at Zabriskie Point, a well-known landmark, from where you can get a panoramic view of Death Valley. Leaving the car in the rocky "car park", we hiked the quarter of a mile steeply up the craggy outcrop. The temperature was 40 degrees centigrade. As we started to take in breaths, the hot air sucked in was burning the roofs of our mouths. We tried to breathe through nose and closed lips. Underfoot it felt like the soles of our sandals were burning. Once at the top we had a magnificent view of the Badlands, as we overlooked Badwater and the Artist's Palette with its different coloured layers of rock. Everywhere was an arid, eroded landscape of rocky plains like the surface of Mars with tortuous gorges, gulleys, crumbling crags and twisted rock formations.

From here we drove the short distance to our lodgings for the night – Furnace Creek Ranch. Furnace Creek Ranch was a desert resort and is known for being the location of the hottest temperature recorded on Earth at 56.7 degrees centigrade or 134 degrees Fahrenheit. In this desert "oasis" there was an 18 hole golf course, two spring fed swimming pools, restaurants, the elegant Inn at Furnace Creek, ranch house units, basketball, volleyball, tennis courts, a General Store and a camp ground. The golf course was known to be the world's lowest, lying at 214 feet below sea level.

We had booked one night's accommodation in the ranch house units. There were four two storey ranch houses built from timber and clad with pebble dash. We had a room on the upper storey at the very end of the building, looking out onto the 18th green of the golf course. Having stowed our luggage, I looked out of the glass door which opened out onto fire escape steps down to the 18th green. It was now late afternoon and all was quiet on the course. I was just making ready to open the door with the purpose of an early evening exploration of the golf course, when a movement to my right demanded my attention. Trotting nonchalantly onto the 18th green, came two coyotes. Having sniffed around the flag, they made off as if headed for the club house. It was then that I decided against an early evening constitutional. Attention was then turned to the room itself and its facilities. A dominant item in the room was an ironing board with iron. When we took some clothing from a case for evening wear, we soon realised the need for the ironing equipment. Clothing from the case, under the intense heat, was more creased than when we'd put it in. The air in the room was hot and stuffy. I touched the wall and withdrew my hand quickly as the burning heat stung me. Examining the air conditioning controls we were warned by a notice that, *"On no account must you turn up the air conditioning otherwise the whole system will fail and it will go off altogether."*

That evening we dined at what could be described as a 1950's American Western Chuck Wagon food place called "The Forty Niner Café". We ate beef burger and chips. It was enough to feed half an English town. After a hot, uncomfortable night's sleep, we set off very early the next morning to avoid the intense heat of the day. With our two gallons of water and sandwiches, cake and coca cola bought at the General Store, we set off on the next leg of the journey with the intention of seeing Badwater and the other features of Death Valley.

We travelled out of Furnace Creek along Highway 190 towards Stovepipe Wells. Passing Badwater, we registered the sign stating that it was 220 feet below sea level, the lowest place in the Western Hemisphere. It was just a vast, shimmering, heat baked desert backed by the distant mountains. The small chemical pools, skirted by salt deposits, shimmered greenish in the harsh sunlight. The brown, green and yellow rock layers of The Artist's Drive amazed us with their unique colour display. En route we stopped to look at the Devil's Golf Course. This was a vast, flat area of salt deposits punctured by chunks of rock. There was a sign saying, *"Turn your air conditioning off!"*

Forking left onto Highway 178, we headed towards Ridgecrest and then onto Highway 14 down to Mojave, turning right onto Highway 58 through Tekachapic, Golden Hills and on to Bakersfield. Once we had crossed Death Valley there were small concreted roads striped with lines of tarmac which had melted and oozed out.

Bakersfield was an unappealing place in the San Joaquin Valley. It was flat, featureless and surrounded by a forest of oil derricks. Passing through Bakersfield, we drove along Interstate 99 towards Fresno where we were to have a short stay before foraying east to sample Sequoia National Park. Passing through Sequoia we were then going to head north to spend several days in Yosemite National Park.

Classic in its ugliness, Fresno is the business centre of the Central Valley. Fresno is economically thriving; a bustling urban centre. It is frequently voted as the least desirable place to live in the U.S. and has the status of being one of the crime hot spots. We were nervous in the knowledge that it was also billed as *"The Gun Capital of the U.S.A."* However, such labels are often an over exaggeration, aren't they? This was our thinking until we reached our hotel. Registering at Reception, we were given a code to the security key pad on our accommodation block. Driving down to the car park, we were convincing ourselves that such security was, after all, a good thing and was there to make the guest feel very safe. Then, we stepped out of the car and saw the two uniformed security guards patrolling either end of the accommodation block. They were armed with automatic weapons.

But, in this unappealing, uneasy environment, there was to be a surprise, a hidden gem that made our stay in Fresno memorable. The Forestiere Underground Gardens. Located at 5021 West Shaw Street, Fresno, this is a hand excavated, a hand built network of underground rooms, patios, caverns, courtyards and passages, reminiscent of the ancient catacombs of Rome only more attractive, more beautiful. This whole network was dug out of the hardpan ground by one man – a Sicilian émigré called Baldassare

Forestiere. Baldassare was a former Boston and New York subway tunneler who arrived in Fresno in 1905.

Arriving at the unassuming entrance, we walked tentatively along a pathway to a covered entrance. It didn't look like the place was open to the public. But suddenly an elderly lady emerged from the grotto – like entrance. Ruth Forestiere welcomed us with gusto and warmth. A relative of Baldassare Forestiere, she was the driving force which kept the place going; she was manager, tour guide, bookkeeper and anything else in order to promote and preserve the site for others to experience. For forty years she had done this and became known as *"The Lady of the Gardens"*. She died on September 12th, 2012. At the beginning of the tour she told us how Forestiere had moved across to Fresno to find employment. He started by living in a wooden shack which Ruth described as being like a "hot, wooden sweat – box" in the hot, clammy Fresno summers. So it was that Baldassare bought ten acres of land in Fresno. But it was unsuitable for growing crops because of the heat and the hardpan soil. Inspired by the ancient catacombs of Rome which he had visited on many occasions during his early life in Europe, Baldassare decided to dig out his own catacombs based on Ancient Roman architecture. He remembered the cool, even temperatures in the catacombs and believed this was the answer to his accommodation. He felt that this would protect him and any crops he wished to grow from the searing heat of the long Fresno summer.

He began to dig out the hardpan using just a shovel and a wheelbarrow. He dug out a labyrinth, a warren of over fifty rooms, passages and other features. He constructed many features from the hardpan, mortar and cement. Walking through this network of underground passages, courtyards and rooms, we came across a parlour with a fire place, a summer and winter bedroom, a courtyard with a bathroom. There was a subterranean bath tub fed by water heated by the midday sun. In a garden court off the kitchen and bedroom there was a small fishpond crossed by a footbridge. The kitchen had all the conveniences then available. In various courtyards there were circular, stone – built planters adorned with shrubs, fruit trees, and vines (some of these are ninety years old). Orange trees growing underground were protected from the winter frosts. Trees and fruits planted included almond, pomegranate, Italian pear, olive, avocado, persimmon, quinoa, carob, fig, tangerine, grapefruit, lemon, date palm, mulberry, kumquat, loquart, and jujube.

Passages and courtyards had open skylights to let in light and air. There are skylights adorned with redwood arbours and pergolas with cascading grapevines. Everywhere there are underground gardens and shrubberies.

In his living areas he built skylights covered in winter with glass to keep out the rain and allow in natural light. He constructed arches, columns, vaulted ceilings carved like inverted tea cups and stonework with scallop – shaped seats carved into walls. All this was adorned with the lush greenery of trees, shrubs and grapevines.

We turned a corner and there, in the courtyard garden, was an aquarium with a circular glass bottom through which tropical fish could be observed.

At every turn there was something unusual, unexpected and wonderful. Here, in Fresno, frequently voted as the least desirable place to live in the U.S.A., was an oasis of beauty, peace, calm and inventiveness, all created by the genius, hard work and vision of one man – Baldassare Forestiere. Baldassare died in 1946.

Leaving Fresno we headed to Yosemite. We duly met up with Colin and Jean and went for a walk through Tuolumne Meadows. The final leg of our journey was from Yosemite to San Francisco. The car rental situation was such that whatever was left in the petrol tank was not refundable. And so we decided that we could reach the car rental garage in San Francisco without refuelling. As we crossed the Bay Bridge the petrol gauge was getting close to empty but we knew we had not far to go. What we didn't factor into our plans was that when you drive into the city streets of San Francisco the one way system meant that you could only turn right. That was no problem as we knew from our maps that we were fast approaching the street where the garage was. We turned right into the street. We were at the bottom end of the street and as we drove we realised that the garage was not in this section. So we took the next right and headed back to where we had turned. The fuel was running out. We passed the first right turn and headed up to the next turning. Turning right we entered the street of our destination. This was the middle section of the street. Still no garage! By now we were getting very worried. Turning right once again we made for the upper section of the street. As we turned into the street we drove down hill and to our relief Ann spotted the garage sign. Twenty yards from the garage the petrol tank was empty and we freewheeled, turning left onto the garage ramp and gliding down to a parking bay just in front of the rental office.

---oOo---

Leaving Delhi on our Indian tour, we were heading for Shimla in the mountains. This was where the British would go to escape the hot summers of the Punjab plains. Up in the mountains close to the foothills of the Himalayas the climate was much cooler and more suited to the British colonials. We were going to Kalka railway station to board the "toy train" for the five hour journey up to Shimla and the Oberon Cecil Hotel.

First, we had to catch a train from Delhi station to Chandigarh. At 6.30 a.m. the journey by bus to the station passed through deserted streets and a hazy atmosphere. As we assembled on the platform we were greeted by a stench. On looking down onto the tracks, it became obvious what was causing it – *human excrement*! There were great piles at intervals between the iron rails.

Boarding carriage number 2 and finding our seats seemed an easy assignment. But no, it did not work out like that! Having settled into seats, one by one our party was accosted by Indians claiming that the seats were theirs. Irate passengers began arguing. The problem was solved when it was realized by our tour guide that we were in the incorrect seats. So everyone had to move to find seats elsewhere.

Passing through rural India on our journey we saw lots of buffalo, dung heaps, people in small shanty – like settlements along the railway track performing their morning toilet ablutions, 'seas' of plastic cartons and bottles mixed in with other rubbish. And rubbish was the theme of the day when we arrived at Chandigarh.

Taking our tour bus from the station we were transferred to the Rock Gardens of Chandigarh. This is a sculpture garden known as Nek Chand's Rock Garden. No one anticipated the marvels we were to see there. The garden was founded by Nek Chand, a government official who started the garden secretly in his spare time in 1957. Chand's work was illegal, but he was able to hide it for 18 years before it was discovered by the authorities in 1975. By this time it had grown to 12 acres. His work was in danger of being demolished, but he was able to get public opinion on his side. In 1976 the park was inaugurated as a public space. Today it is spread over 40 acres and is completely built of industrial and home waste and thrown – away items.

The garden houses sculptures made by using a variety of different, discarded waste materials like frames, mudguards, forks, handlebars, metal wires, porcelain, auto parts, plastic bottles, broken, colorful glass bangles, discarded rubber tyres etc. He created figurines and statues, mud and cement animals such as bears, monkeys, horses. With a work force of fifty labourers, under the title of "Sub-Divisional Engineer, Rock Garden", he continued to create new work adding soothing waterfalls washing over statues made of broken ceramic tiles of all colours. He created passages cooled by high walls lined with mosaics of broken ceramics which led into mosaic courtyards and deep gorges. Doorways and archways constructed from discarded bags of cement, led to new and wonderful sculptures.

The Rock Garden is a complex labyrinth with pathways, gateways, steps, waterfalls, courtyards, porches and buildings. Nek Chand created open courtyards decorated with sculptures, complete with the king's and queen's chambers. A large waterfall, a canal, an open air theatre, a miniature village and fairground, are also included. These spaces have become interactive areas where plays, dance and music performances are held. Life sized horses and camels have been moulded from waste. The Rock Garden consists of at least 5000 sculptures. It is truly an unusual and wonderful place which you do not expect as you enter through the main gateway. It is akin to the Forestiere Underground Gardens but on a much bigger scale.

The Chandigarh Rock Garden is now acknowledged as one of the modern wonders of the world.

8. Sake, Sashimi, Noodles, Vodka, Andouillette and other Delicacies

One aspect of different cultures is cuisine. Food and drink play a big part in any holiday. Local delicacies can be sampled, but sometimes, you don't always get what you expect.

We journeyed to Japan with our friends Mike and Margaret. Their eldest son, Liam, had been working there in Japanese schools as a teacher of English. Having met Mika, a Japanese girl, he was getting married. Arriving in Tokyo we looked forward to the Shinto wedding which was to take place in a Shinto temple shrine.

Before the wedding we went to see Fujiyama, The Sacred Mountain, on the Shinkansen, or Bullet Train. On the station platform the electronic timetable told us that the next train was due in 2 minutes 20 seconds. In precisely 2 minutes 20 seconds, the Bullet Train drew up quietly alongside the platform. We journeyed through the built up suburbs of Tokyo until we were speeding through the countryside towards Nagoya, Kyoto and Osaka. As we went a snow capped Fujiyama came into view. Disembarking at Shin Fuji station, we strolled through the streets with the mountain as our backdrop. We went on a boat trip on Lake Ashinoko, where we got splendid views of Fujiyama. An active volcano, Mount Fuji at 12,388 feet, last erupted in 1708.

The next day was to be the wedding. Gathering outside the shrine, Liam and Mika appeared in traditional Japanese dress, she in a white ceremonial kimono, he in a black kimono. The ceremony began. Rituals were performed which we did not understand.

Then, sitting on wooden bench seats, the congregation was asked to stand. Each one of us was presented with a silver plated "degustation" type spoon. One of the temple officials came round with a silver ewer and poured water into each person's spoon, including the bride and groom. The bride and groom drank from their spoons. On a signal the congregation toasted them by downing the contents of their spoons. It was only as the liquid slipped down our throats with a burning sensation that we realised we had not toasted the "happy couple" with water but with sake. The wedding meal followed with sushi and traditional Japanese cuisine – very tasty but with no further surprises.

However, later in the week, when Mike and Margaret went to dine with Mika's family, we found our way to a local restaurant. The menu was in

Japanese but was accompanied with pictures of the meals. Presented with the menu it took us some time to decide what was what. We thought we had deciphered what was on offer and chose several fish and meat dishes and two bowls of noodles to accompany them. We showed the waiter the pictures of the dishes we wanted and indicated one of each for both of us. He went away looking puzzled. Within a minute he came back and pointed to each item in the picture, trying to indicate something to us. Of course we could not understand what he was saying. In the end he showed us each dish we had ordered and asked if we wanted it indicating with a shake or nod of the head. We nodded in the affirmative to each dish. That's what we wanted. The waiter retreated. A minute later he returned. Someone had armed him with the words "yes" and "no". Once again we answered in the affirmative. Looking defeated, bewildered and disbelieving, the waiter bowed slightly and retreated backwards.

Sipping beers, we fiddled with the chopsticks, trying them out. Soon the waiter reappeared, depositing dishes of meat and fish. Each one looked appetizing. Just as we were expressing our opinions doubting all the fuss the waiter had made, he reappeared with two bowls of noodles and placed them next to one of the meat dishes. Two bowls of noodles. No problem. I pushed one bowl towards my wife and took one myself. Picking up chopsticks, we stopped suddenly as the waiter appeared with two more bowls of noodles, placing them next to one of the fish dishes. Slightly surprised we had no time to start eating when he appeared with another two bowls of noodles, placing them by the other fish dish.

Appearing for a final time, he brought the last two bowls of noodles, placing them separately to the rest of the food. Eight bowls of noodles! Shaking our heads, we made a start on our noodle banquet. Taking a break from a mouthful of cold noodles, I looked up to see the waiter standing at one side with another waiter and one of the chefs. They watched us with great interest, intrigued by the English liking for cold noodles. Obviously we did not finish all the noodles. But we did realize that the waiter had been trying to tell us that each dish came with a bowl of noodles for each person.

That wasn't the end of our Japanese gourmet experiences. Joining the whole of our wedding party one evening, we went to a local restaurant for Teppanyaki. We sat on cushions around low, sunken tables. In the centre of each table were small hobs, heated from below by candles. Plates of vegetables were spread around and then each table was furnished with dishes of raw meat strips. Cooking, barbecue style, on the hobs, we enjoyed a delicious feast. When the youngsters in the party, on the following evening, decided on a pub crawl with a McDonald's feast thrown in, we four adults went to another small, local restaurant. Looking at the number of bewildering items on the menus, it was suggested that we had the sharing sashimi ika platter. We had already sampled sushi and various raw fish dishes such as tuna which we had enjoyed. We were looking forward to the platter. The large dish was placed in the centre of the table. Chopsticks were at the ready. We picked up pieces of raw fish and put them onto our plates uncovering four whole baby squid. Each had long tentacles and was white tinged with purple. I looked at them warily. They reminded me of "just born" baby birds which had fallen from their nest, lying on the ground with purple skin and blind eyes. I was staring at the unappetising morsels when Margaret picked one up, popped it whole into her mouth, eating it with obvious pleasure.

'Absolutely delicious,' she said, savouring every moment.

Then Mike picked up his baby squid, held it in the chopsticks in front of his face and said, 'Would you like another, love?' Margaret accepted it gleefully.

A minute later Ann said, 'Do you fancy mine?'

Not to be outdone and worried that I would be left to try the delicacy, I added quickly, 'You can have mine as well.'

The three of us sat and watched as Margaret ate the four raw baby squids. She really enjoyed them and couldn't understand that we did not want them.

Of course, ika, in Japanese, meant squid.

---oOo---

A tour of South America to Peru, Bolivia, Argentina and Brazil introduced us to other exotic and unusual foods.

From Lima, in Peru, we flew to Cuzco in the Andes to acclimatise for our visit to Machu Picchu. In order to cope with the thinner atmosphere of Cuzco at an altitude of 11,000 feet, we were advised at our hotel to partake of "afternoon tea". But this wasn't coffee, Earl Grey or English Breakfast tea with cucumber sandwiches and cakes. It was a brew of coca leaves.

Depositing a few coca leaves into a cup, we poured hot water onto them, added a spoonful of sugar and sipped. Coca tea, also called mate de coca, is an herbal tea infusion made using the raw leaves of the coca plant. It is greenish yellow in colour and has a mild, bitter flavour. The leaves of the coca plant contain alkaloids which, when extracted chemically, are the source for cocaine base. It is a mild stimulant which is reckoned to suppress the nausea and headaches associated with altitude sickness. The coca alkaloid content of coca tea is such that the consumption of one cup can cause a positive result on a drug test for cocaine! Coca tea is legal in Columbia, Peru, Bolivia, Argentina, Ecuador and Chile. However, coca tea is illegal in the United States but has been used to wean cocaine addicts off the drug. That night I was unable to sleep. If I lay flat I couldn't get my breath. I had to try and sleep propped up against the pillow. Was it altitude sickness or the coca tea?

Once acclimatised, we set off on a trip to Sacsayhuaman. The guide told us that the easiest way to pronounce this was "sexywoman". It was a magical, mysterious site on a gigantic scale. The giant, multi – faceted stonework was unbelievable. Giant slabs lay on top of each other without mortar and with joins that were hardly visible. Llamas and alpacas roamed freely across the site. There is a section where you can slide down as the Incas did. Off to one side of the main site is a cliff top crowned with a large cross. This was to mark the visit of John Paul II to Peru.

The next morning we set off on a coach into the Sacred Valley, the Urumbamba valley, to see various

Inca ruins on our journey to Machu Picchu. We stopped at Ollantaytambo to visit the temple ruins. We walked up the great tiered construction with its fantastic Inca architecture and carvings. The inhabitants of these settlements in the Sacred Valley were Quechura speaking. It was when visiting one small village that we were allowed to wander in and out of the small homesteads. Walking into the gloom of one dwelling we were aware of a scrabbling, scratching noise and high pitched squeaking. Once our eyes were used to the dimness, we could see where the noises were coming from. One half of the stone floor was covered with straw and, scuttering about in it were at least a hundred guinea pigs. Scattered amongst the straw were nuts and seeds. One of our group was wondering why they would keep so many pets when they could barely scrape a living for themselves. Hearing this on entering behind us, our tour guide explained that they weren't pets; that they were a source of food, a delicacy for these villagers; and that many were headed for the markets in Lima, Cuzco and other places to end up on restaurant menus. Indeed, later on, when we had returned to Cuzco and went to dine in a restaurant, guinea pig was on the menu. My wife and I both resisted the desire to order guinea pig. Instead I ordered alpaca!

From these villages we drove to a small railway station. From here the train ran to its terminus at Aguas Calientes, a frontier town nestled below Machu Picchu. Taking the local Machu Piccuh bus we went up the spiralling and precipitous road which wound all the way up to the café and shop on the threshold of the ancient Inca town. From the shop we walked the short distance up into the ruins of Machu

Piccuh. We held our breaths as we witnessed wonderful view after wonderful view. This was a truly remarkable place and fit to rival the Seven Ancient Wonders of the World.

---oOo---

France is often hailed as the gastronomic capital of the world. But even in places with such a glowing reputation, you can come across a diabolic dining experience. You might add that the waiter who served us on that perversely memorable occasion was the Devil's Advocate.

From the farmhouse in the remote countryside somewhere just north of the Loire, where the Bat Incident had occurred, the four of us drove to Saumur intent on dining out at one of the many restaurants there. However, we were unaware of the fact that it was a Saints Day or a Feast Day, in fact a French public holiday. Passing restaurant after restaurant which were closed for the holiday, we wandered into a large square. Pigeons fluttered past us and landed, scavenging for morsels to eat, but nowhere was there a human to be seen. Crossing the square, we were about to abandon our dining plans and head back to the "Bat House" to dine on bread, cheese and beer. But fate intervened. If only it hadn't!

Pointing in excitement, we spotted, in the far corner of the square, tables set with check table cloths outside a small restaurant which appeared to have its doors open. Striding urgently we reached the restaurant. It was like the *Marie Celeste*. Nobody to be seen. No customers dining outside or inside. Turning, we were about to retrace our steps across the square, when a small figure appeared inside the restaurant. The waiter, dressed in long white apron stained with old, encrusted food, came outside towards us. Trotting at his side was a rather large Alsatian dog. Patting the dog's head, he stood looking at us with enquiring eyes. He was short, with an unkempt black moustache and hair, and was wearing dirty, faded trousers and brown shoes which had never seen polish and looked battered and worn. But, in our desperation to have lunch, we ignored all the signs; the dog, the appearance of the waiter, the absence of customers. After all, this was real, ethnic dining, about which many a misguided British tourist would boast. In our most fluent French we said "Ouvert? Ouvert?" With a Gallic shrug and a sweep of his arm he replied, "Oui." The dog said nothing. Then, before we could make an assessment of the situation, he guided us to a table, scurried off inside, and returned with menus.

We ordered salads and a main dish each. But my wife, Ann, always the adventurous diner, ordered andouillettes. Cumberland sausages, salami, pork and cider sausages were all enjoyed by Ann. Of course andouillettes are sausages. As we sat sipping beers, the first manifestation of our mistake was highlighted, when Ann exclaimed, 'I don't believe it! Would you just look at that?' And so we did. What did we see? Inside the restaurant, waiting for the salads, the waiter was busily patting the Alsatian's head and stroking him vigorously. As we looked, the dog's long salivating tongue was licking the waiter's hands comprehensively. Then, suddenly, the waiter turned away from the dog as two large bowls of salad appeared on the kitchen hatch. Putting them onto a tray, he crossed the room, picking pieces of lettuce, pepper and tomato from the plates and popping them into his mouth as he went. Grunting and sniffing, he plonked them unceremoniously onto the table. We looked at the salads, and we looked at each other, our faces contorted in disbelief and disgust. Retreating into the restaurant, he sat at a table. The Alsatian stood on its haunches with its paws and head on the waiter's lap, continuing to lick his hands and face as he ruffled its fur. Nobody touched the salads. Soon two fish dishes and one veal escalope were delivered. It was then that Ann noticed the dirt under the waiter's fingernails. Returning, he slapped down the plate of andouillettes. The pale, almost transparent skin of the andouillettes looked disgusting. Cutting the end off one, we all peered at the pulpy, knotted innards. It was then that we realised that these were sausages made from pork and veal intestines or chitterlings mixed with tripe, diced peppers and onions. In fact, the greatest andouillette delicacy is to use the colon of the animal.

Ann simply put her knife and fork down. The smell, the appearance, the lack of restaurant ambience, or should I say hygiene, was too much. This was not so much Michelin Star but more Michelin Tyre. Ann shared a little of my veal escalope but all of us picked at the food, quickly abandoning it and leaving it unfinished. Rather than complain to a waiter who wouldn't understand or care, we simply asked for "l'addition", paid it and left as quickly as possible.

---oOo---

An eightieth birthday celebration in St. Petersburg, Russia, resulted in a different kind of indulgence. Our eldest son, Steven, was married to a Russian girl, Natascha, or as she was known by her family, Natalia. Having lived in Leeds for a number of years, Steven and Natascha were travelling to St. Petersburg to celebrate her grandma's or Baboushka's eightieth birthday. My wife and I were invited too.

On passing through the crowded St. Petersburg airport, we headed for the baggage reclaim. Standing in front of the carousel trying to identify our luggage, we were suddenly alarmed as a tap on the shoulder was followed by, 'No! No! Not any need! See, over here.'

As we all turned round, we were surprised to see Natascha's father, Vladimir, standing there, hands on hips, in the Baggage Reclaim!

'Come, come! We have the luggage. My chauffeur already is taking your bags to the car.'

Following Vladimir, we strode outside where the chauffeur was already loading our luggage. There were two cars, one driven by Vladimir, the other by his chauffeur. We went with the chauffeur. Steven and Natascha went with her father. Making sure that we were settled into our hotel, Steven and Natascha left with Vladimir to his apartment.

That evening we were invited to go to the apartment and dine with the family. Steven came to collect us and we travelled the short distance on the underground Metro beneath the River Neva. Stepping from the roadway, we walked beneath an archway which led into an inner courtyard. Just inside there was an ancient looking lift. It had heavy metal trellis gates. Steven pulled these open revealing the heavy, rusting metal doors of the lift. Pressing a button we heard a motor stutter into life. We could see the huge oiled cables which lowered the lift to ground level. Once inside the metal cage another button was pressed and the heavy doors groaned then clanged shut. The lift rose slowly up the short distance to first floor level. Here, we stepped out onto the concrete landing. To our left was a huge, studded, metal door. Steven pressed the button on a small intercom and spoke into it. Thirty seconds later we heard what sounded like a door opening on the other side of the metal door. Then, lurching and creaking, the heavy metal door slowly opened. Standing on the threshold was a smiling Vladimir. We were welcomed with kisses on both cheeks and ushered inside. It was then that we could see that there was a heavy, wood panelled door which was just behind the metal door. As we edged into a gloomy hall space, the two doors were shut firmly. It was explained that the outer metal door was a security feature. I imagine that soldiers with hand held missile launchers would be unable to breach these fortifications.

We were led into a large living room with a thick piled carpet sporting swirling, russet patterns. There were heavily bossed and gilded mirrors on the wall and various religious icons. The large table stood in the middle covered in a dark blue tablecloth and already set for dinner. Wallpaper was bold with grey blue geometric motif on a beige background. A heavy chandelier cast a deep glow, bathing the room in a diffused, orange light.

Natascha introduced us to Baboushka and we greeted each other in the usual Russian embrace.

Soon after exchanging pleasantries, Olga, Natascha's mother disappeared through the hall space, where we had entered, into the kitchen. In addition, at the rear of the apartment, there were two bedrooms. Having been seated at the table, the two ladies appeared with steaming bowls of Borsche. Next we had chicken legs and wings with potatoes and salad. Then we had pieces of cold sturgeon and salmon followed by a desert of blueberry crumble. Throughout the meal we were regaled with shots of the purest Russian vodka. This was the precursor of what was to come the next evening at Baboushka's eightieth birthday party.

Having returned to our hotel after sampling the hospitality of a typical Russian family we found it difficult to sleep. Night did not seem to come. In fact, it did not come. It was June and it was the *White Nights*, when it was permanently twenty four hours of daylight.

The next day we were taken to Senate Square and the hermitage Museum. Then we returned to the hotel to get ready for the evening's eightieth birthday party.

We were driven in a minibus to a city centre restaurant. The party was downstairs in a vaulted - ceiling cellar. Drinks were followed by a three course meal accompanied by a guitarist. Between courses Baboushka and her mother Olga joined the guitarist and together they sang a traditional Russian song. As the final course reached its end Vladimir stood up, banged a spoon on the table, cleared his throat and addressed the thirty guests seated around the table in Russian. He then explained in English that the tradition at a Russian birthday party was for each person to say a few words about the person whose birthday it was and then propose a toast.

Natascha's mum sat by Ann and me with a vodka bottle and three vodka shot glasses. The first person said something about Baboushka. Everyone clapped then the person raised their glass full of vodka and proposed a toast. Everyone, including us, stood and downed the vodka in one. This procedure was repeated thirty times as each guest in turn spoke and then proposed a toast. Olga made sure that we downed each glass in one and then refilled the glasses ready for the next toast. Thirty vodka shots later, at the end of the party, we climbed back into the minibus feeling somewhat disorientated and giggling at every opportunity. Later, as we settled back into our hotel room, we were fearful of what painful hangover would pay us back the following morning.

The next morning we woke fresh and ready for the day with no after effects at all. There is something to be said for the purest Russian vodka! Our stay in St. Petersburg included visits to the Peter and Paul Fort where we saw, in the church, the tombs of the Romanovs; the magnificent creation of Peter the Great at the stunning Peterof; the unique Amber Room at St. Catherine Palace; shopping along Nevsky Prospect; and the ornate Church of The Spilt Blood covered inside with the colourful, mosaic frescos of biblical events.

---oOo---

Having crossed the border from Vietnam into Cambodia, our tour group was travelling on a bus to Siem Reap. Siem Reap was to be our base for our long awaited visit to Anghor Wat. We travelled along a very bumpy road, one section being a complete dirt track. Dust billowed in clouds creating the effect of being in a sandstorm. As we went we noticed that many of the houses in Cambodia tended to be built on stilts because of flooding.

To break our journey we stopped at a place called Stuon at an open air market. All kinds of foodstuffs were being sold. Walking through the stalls we noticed some frightening looking specimens. They looked like spiders. Our tour guide, Jesse James, who was originally from Barrow – in – Furness but had lived for the past eight years in Cambodia, came up behind us with a broad smile on his face. Swishing his pony tail he said,'They're a local delicacy round here. Fried insects and scorpions and those fried tarantulas. Come with me and have a look.' Jesse led us over to the corner of a building. Here he pointed out a polystyrene box with a lid. The lid had been slid to one side. We could see that there were things moving, crawling and climbing out of the box. It was a box full of baby tarantulas. A young Cambodian child, still in a nappy, about eighteen months old, was squatting by the box, happily playing with the tarantulas. They crawled over his hands and moved along his arms. If any fell out of the box he picked them up and put them back in.

Travelling on, we detoured to the village of Kampong Lang. Twenty thousand people lived here along the shores of Toule Sap Lake. This was a village with dusty and muddy "roads" and houses on stilts. The stilts must have been 20-30 feet high, an indication of how high the floods could rise. On foot we walked along the rutted dirt tracks until we came to a wooden swing bridge. Crossing the bridge, we travelled through the "streets" witnessing life at its most basic. The houses were made from bamboo poles with walls and roofs of woven palm leaves. Babies peeped out of doorways, people fished along the edge of the river, others went about their daily business. Fishermen were paddling into the lake on long, shallow hulled, wooden boats. Using metal baskets they were scooping out fresh water shrimps and many fish. Others on land were smoking fish. We arrived at a local house and climbed the wide, wooden stairs. Squatting on the floor, around the edge of two large rugs, we were served chicken soup, vegetables, fish, rice, omelettes, pineapple and lychees, a can of beer for just six dollars.

9. When Irish Eyes are Smiling

Trips to Ireland are always joyful and refreshing. Our first holiday with two friends was to the south east of Ireland – to County Wexford. Driving down from the ferry at Dun Laoghaire, Dublin, we called in at Avoca, the village which bore the fictional name of Ballykissangel in the T.V. series. Reaching the south east coast, looking out onto St. George's Channel, we took up residence on a small housing estate in the seaside village of Dunmore East in County Wexford. Having had a gourmet meal at the local restaurant looking out onto the bay, we settled into our modern holiday home.

The next day we planned a drive westwards through Waterford and on towards Cork, paying a visit to

Blarney Castle. On the road to Waterford we passed a thatched cottage and stopped in front of it to check our route. By the large oak door there was a board and neatly written in white capital letters we read: *Kennedys. Licensed to sell alcohol.* There was no pub sign or car park or indeed any other indication that this might be a pub. We decided that we would explore this on our return trip.

Once we had negotiated Waterford we found ourselves alone on the road westwards. Mile after mile we travelled with no one in front or behind us. After a while we encountered a tractor. The tractor pulled over to the side immediately to let us past.

Arriving at the site of Blarney Castle, we parked our car and went into the compulsory shop. The large lady shop owner watched our every move. The two wives both selected something from the array of souvenirs and craft items. A discussion broke out about who was going to kiss the Blarney Stone. It turned out that I was the only one wishing to do so. As the wives bought their goods from the shopkeeper I asked her if there was a charge to kiss the Blarney Stone. She replied, 'There is, sure. One punt. But why you be needing to do that, I don't know. For sure, don't you be having enough of the Gift of the Gab already?'

Blarney Castle is five miles from Cork. The Blarney Stone is a block of carboniferous limestone built into the battlements of the castle. It is said that it was set into the tower of the castle in 1446.The story relates that Cormac Laidir McCarthy, the builder of Blarney Castle, was involved in a lawsuit. He appealed to the goddess Cliodhna for help. She told him to kiss the first stone he found in the morning on his way to court. He did so and pleaded his case with such great eloquence that he won. Thus the stone was said to impart "the ability to deceive without offending." McCarthy incorporated it into the battlements of the castle. There are many such legends and stories. Another story describes how the stone was presented to McCarthy by Robert the Bruce in 1314 in recognition of his support in the Battle of Bannockburn. Legend says it was a piece of the Stone of Scone but this was not known about at that time.

I climbed the steps up onto the battlements whilst the rest of my party looked on from the safety of "terra firma". Two men were crouched by a gap in the turreting. When my turn arrived a hand stretched out and I put the punt (no euros in those days) into it. Then I had to lie flat on my back over a gap in the edge of the parapet. The parapet was fitted with vertical, wrought iron guide rails. I reached up and grabbed hold of them as firmly as I could. My head and upper torso dangled over the edge. Just below me were two horizontal protective crossbars. One assistant held onto me and the other sat astride my legs. I leant back and kissed the stone which was set into the battlement wall just above my head.

After visiting Cork we set off on our return journey. Passing through Waterford we headed along the road to East Dunmore, pulling up outside the thatched cottage which we thought was a pub. The board still had *Kennedys. Licensed to sell alcohol* fixed to the wall next to the door. The large, oak door was still firmly shut and there was no sign of life inside or even along the road outside. I was sent ahead like the raven from Noah's Ark to "test the water". Gingerly, I pressed down the latch and pushed. The door was not locked. Slowly it swung open. I stepped into the gloom and, as the light flooded in from behind me, I saw a square room with a stone flagged floor. Along both edges were wooden seats – like pews and scattered along them were small, round tables with old, wooden chairs. Looking to my left I then saw the bar counter with three or four hand pulled pumps. Across the room an old man, all by himself, holding a pint of Guinness, looked at me quizzically and then, ignoring my entrance, began to sip the drink. Suddenly, a middle aged lady, wearing an apron, came through an open door to the right of the bar. Holding two plates of food in her hands, she crossed the room. Nervously I asked, 'Are you open?'

'Sure we are,' she replied. 'Take yourself a seat. I'll be back in a moment.'

Popping my head around the door, I beckoned to the others and we all sat down round a small table. The barmaid reappeared from a room at the other side of the bar. As she shut the door behind her we could hear the squabbling voices of children.

'Ah, there you are. Just had to give the children their tea. Now, let's be seeing what you'd like.'

The two husbands approached the bar and said, 'Two pints of Guinness and two halves.'

'That's a good choice.'

'We didn't know if you were open,' said Joe, our friend. 'What time do you open?'

'Oh, all the time. Whenever you like- oh - er – except that is, between three and half past. That's when I get the children from school.'

'The door was shut so we thought you might not be open,' I said.

'Don't you be worrying about that. The door's always closed. Just push it open and come in any time. Ah, even if it's locked, and you be wanting a drink just give a good knock and we'll let you in.'

The barmaid, mother, proprietor placed two pints and two halves of Guinness on the counter. I went to pick one up and the lady slapped my wrist.

'Just be leaving that there. It's got to settle before I top it up. Be sitting down and I'll bring them over to you.'

Not being Guinness drinkers we were determined to sample the brew having been told by many people that Guinness in Ireland is not like Guinness served anywhere else and that it is a really smooth and satisfying drink. How right this turned out to be. The drink was like black nectar and we thoroughly enjoyed it and several more before we finished out holiday.

.

---oOo---

Another Irish trip was to South West Ireland – County Kerry. Landing at Shannon airport with two friends we hired a car and set off southwards from Limerick. We arrived at our hotel in Killarney with plans to drive the Ring of Kerry.

We drove the Ring of Kerry where the scenery was breathtaking and beautiful. But the highlight of our stay was a trip through the Gap of Dunloe. Hiring the old fashioned "Gap of Dunloe and Lakes of Killarney Adventure" bus or charabanc, we set off from Killarney Main Street to Ros Castle on the shores of Lough Leane.

Ros Castle (Caislean an Rois in Irish) is a fifteenth century tower house and keep on the edge of Lough Leane in the Killarney National Park. It was the ancestral home of the O'Donoghue clan but more recently owned by the Brownes of Killarney. The legend states that O'Donoghue leaped or was sucked out of the window of the grand chamber at the top of the castle. He disappeared into the lake along with his horse, table and library. It is said he now lives in a great palace at the bottom of the lake where he keeps a close eye on everything that he sees.

From the shores of Lough Leane, at the small pier close to Ros Castle, we boarded the small, wooden boat with about eight other people and two bicycles. Firing up the Yamaha outboard motor, the boatman took the tiller and we sailed out across the Lower Lake. Soon we reached the twin arches of the Old

Weir stone bridge. Here the water was very choppy and the current rushed towards us. It is known as "The Meeting of the Waters" where the river Gearhameen powers its way from the Middle and Upper Lakes into the Lower Lake. The boat struggled against the current as it headed towards the bridge. The boatman, having scanned his passengers, turned to me and my friend Lewis, and shouted above the whine of the outboard and the surge of water, 'I be needing two strong, young men to help me in a few minutes. Are you O.K. with that?' We nodded yes. Our two wives looked concerned. It was only then that, looking round the boat, that we realized we were, in our sixties, the youngest on board.

'When I pull in I want yous two to grab those ropes there, jump out and pull tight on them to secure us and keep the boat as still as possible.'

The boat spluttered and struggled against the current. Then the boatman guided the boat to the rocky bank of the river. He shouted to us, 'Out you get an' hold tight on the tow ropes!' Lewis and I jumped out taking the strain on the ropes. The boatman told all the other passengers to get out, walk over the Old Weir Bridge and wait on the opposite bank.

'Right ho, lads. It be too shallow ahead for the motor. I want yous to tow the boat with the ropes as soon as I lift the outboard and shout "now!" '

We walked along the slippery rock bank until our ropes were taut. It took a great effort to stop the boat surging back with the current. Then the boatman turned off the motor, lifted it clear of the water, took hold of the tiller and shouted, 'Now lads. Pull her along to the deeper water.'

Straining against the power of the current, we took small steps forward. After a huge effort the boat began to move upstream. Stepping in a small pool of water in the smooth hollow of a flat rock, my foot slipped and I was down on my knees. Immediately the tow rope slackened and the boat began to move backwards in the clutches of the current. Lewis stood his ground and pulled hard on the tow rope. The boatman shouted, 'Keep pulling or we'll be back under t'Old Weir Bridge.'

I jammed my foot against a rock which jutted from the bank. The boat held still. Then I scrambled to my feet. With one last surge of energy we pulled and the boat began to move again upstream.

'That's it! Hold her there lads.'

With ropes now wrapped around our waists we stood our ground. The boatman lowered the outboard and powered up the motor. The boat, now in deeper water, surged forward a little.

'Throw yer ropes in an' get in yersels,' shouted the boatman. With tow ropes back in the hull and the two of us safely seated, the boat headed across the river to the far bank. There, the rest of the passengers clambered aboard and we set off up the river on our journey towards the Upper Lake.

What a journey it was! The river cut and wound its way through beautiful water meadows adorned with every colour of wild flower. In the near distance, on the right, were the rounded hills and higher peaks of the Tomies and the Purple Mountains. On the left was the majestic sight of Torch Mountain. It was a truly mesmerizing and relaxing journey.

After a while we entered the Upper Lake and docked at Lord Brandon's Cottage where we had refreshments. From there we entered the awe inspiring Gap of Dunloe, a pass which wound its way between towering peaks. Three of us set off on foot on the seven mile walk through the Gap. My wife, Ann, went on the Jaunting Cart – a unique, brightly painted trap pulled by one horse. Our journey ended at the other side of the Gap of Dunloe. As we arrived on foot we found Ann sitting outside Kate Kearney's Cottage waiting with well-deserved pints of cold beer. When the old charabanc arrived we were driven back to Killarney.

---oOo---

From Killarney we travelled south to the small town of Kenmare at the head of Kenmare Bay on Kenmare River. Kenmare lies between the peninsulas of The

Ring of Kerry and The Ring of Beara. Lying to the south of this is Bantry Bay. Kenmare (Ceann Mara) means "head of the sea". We were staying in a modern holiday home on a small estate. Whilst based here we drove The Ring of Beara and visited Bantry Bay.

It was a warm, sunny day when we went for a local walk up through woods and over hillsides. This was a circular walk from the road and returning to the road. As we finished the walk along the road we passed a line of semi – detached houses. As we approached one particular house we saw an elderly lady on the pavement wielding shears and clipping away at a small, bushy tree bordering her neighbour's drive. Seeing us approach she stopped for a rest.

'Good morning to yous,' she said.

We slowed down and stopped.

'You've got a big job there,' one of us said.

'Ah, it's not so bad. I can manage except for going up this here stepladder to reach the very tops. I'm not a good one with heights these days. But I must be doing it. You see, it's not me own tree. It's his next door but t'poor soul's in hospital you see.'

'Oh dear, did he have a heart attack or something?' said one of the ladies.

'Be Jeez, no! Poor ol' soul left 'is gas stove on. One spark an' it blew up. He was blown out the back door. He's recovering well now but it all made a mess of his kitchen. So I'm helping him out by trimming his tree. He normally likes to keep it tidy. But it's getting' a bit on t'warm side now an' I'm not as sprite as I used to be.'

'Do you want us to give you a hand?' volunteered Lewis. 'I can see what needs cutting back at the top.'

'Ah now, I couldn't be troublin' yous. You're all on holiday, I be guessing.

'Yes. And Kenmare's a beautiful place,' I said.

'It's no trouble,' said Lewis. 'You shouldn't be going up those ladders. Look, we can be up there and trim it off, no trouble.'

'But I can't be spoilin' your holiday.'

'We've finished our walk. We're only in the holiday houses down the road,' I said. 'We'd like to help.'

'Oh, Mother of Mercy, would you? You're angels sent by Hissel' '

So Lewis went up the ladder chopping and cutting back branches and twigs whilst I held the ladder steady. After a while the old lady said, 'That's a good job. That'll do. You've done enough an'...'

'Got to get those very top ones to tidy it off.'

'Oh, you're all Good Christian Folk. May the Mother of Jesus bless you.'

As Lewis clambered down from the ladder we began to gather the fallen leaves and twigs.

'No, no. I'll be doin' that. You good folks have done enough. You'll leave nothin' for an old lady to do. Thank you. Thank you. An' I hope you'll all have the best of holidays.'

Having said our goodbyes, we set off down the road.

10. Animal Antics

Touring the countries of South America, including Peru, Bolivia and Argentina, we arrived at our final destination – Brazil. Walking the track alongside the mighty Iguassu Falls, which straddled the Brazil – Argentina border, we witnessed a truly awe inspiring natural phenomenon. The Falls are formed where the Iguassu River tumbles over the edge of the Parana Plateau. The word Iguassu comes from the Guarani or Tupi words "y" meaning "water" and "uasu" meaning "big". Legend has it that a deity planned to marry the beautiful woman Naipi but she fled with her mortal lover Taroba in a canoe. In a rage the deity sliced the river creating waterfalls and condemning the lovers to an eternal fall. At heights ranging from 60 to 82 metres it is higher than Niagara Falls which is 50 metres at its highest. Upon seeing Iguassu Falls, US First Lady, Eleanor Roosevelt, reportedly exclaimed, "Poor Niagara". With a total width of 2.7 kilometers, Iguassu is wider than Victoria Falls but is split into many falls and islands. Victoria Falls has the largest single curtain of water at more than 1600 meters. A large amount of water is thrust down Devil's Throat, a long chasm that is 82 meters high, 150 meters wide and 700 meters long.

Visiting the Brazilian side of the fall, we set off along the special walkways which ran above the canyon. We had not gone very far when we came to a small kiosk and café. Standing next to a litter bin I got a sudden shock. First of all a canister jumped up from the bin and landed at my feet. This was rapidly followed by a continuous shower of litter. Lollipop wrappers, empty plastic water bottles, polystyrene containers, cigarette packets and polythene wrappings all erupted from the litter bin and scattered onto the walkway. Had there been some kind of earth tremor, I wondered? Then rustling and scratching was followed by a rodent like head which peeped over the top of the litter bin. The long snout and white bespectacled eyes were topped by small ears. It was a raccoon-like creature. A long, striped, curling tail suddenly shot up vertically. Soon the whole animal was visible. It stared at me with black, beady eyes, leapt from the litter bin and ambled nonchalantly along the edges of the path, sniffing here and there, seeking out any morsel of food it could find. It was, in fact, a coati. Coatis are about the size of a large house cat but can have large, sharp canine teeth. They have bear and raccoon-like paws and walk *plantigrade* (on the soles of the feet, as do humans).

Having spent an overnight stay at Iguassu, we travelled on northwards to Rio de Janeiro. Staying in a hotel just behind the main Copacabana stretch, we visited the many sights of Rio, including Sugar Loaf Mountain, the site of the Rio Carnival and the impressive statue of Christ the Redeemer.

To visit Christ the Redeemer we boarded a small train which ran up the Corcovado Mountain to the very foot of the statue. We had to wait at a halt where the double track ended and continued up the mountain on a single track. Awaiting the descending train, we looked out onto the lush vegetation alongside the track which was bejewelled with multi-coloured exotic wild flowers. We were looking out of the window at these flowers when, suddenly, a humming bird fluttered in front of us, hovering in midair, its long beak lapping the nectar from the flower heads with its tongue. Transfixed we watched this for over five minutes. Its head shone an iridescent green and its gorget or neck area was bright blue. Flapping its orange tipped wing feathers very rapidly, the rest of its green breast feathers sparkled in the sunlight. The approach of the descending train disturbed the humming bird and it darted away. The moment of magic ended.

Arriving at the upper station, we climbed the steps up onto the pedestal, thronged with hundreds of tourists. Shining white in the sunlight, the statue towered above us. Christ the Redeemer, with arms outstretched, was a truly memorable sight.

We had anticipated and expected the awe inspiring sights of the natural phenomenon of the Iguassu Falls and the man-made beauty of Christ the Redeemer but the bonus was the unexpected magic created by a foraging coati and the hovering beauty of one small humming bird.

---oOo---

Having visited the Taj Mahal (India), we left the Agra Hotel at 9.15. Travelling through the streets on the coach we saw all sorts of sights. Four people clinging onto motorbikes (including children); donkeys carrying bricks; barbers plying their trade in the streets; chickens stacked in baskets balancing on the backs of bicycles; fridges loaded onto bicycles; and cow patties drying by the roadside in order to be used for fuel for cooking.

On leaving Agra we came upon some people carrying flags. They were on their way to the Chrishtiyya Shrine at Fatehphur Sikri. This was a Muslim festival and pilgrimage. Further along the road the few became hundreds, the hundreds became thousands and the thousands became tens of thousands. Their destination was about 25 miles away. All along the road where they were walking in never ending procession, were marquees or covered areas where the travellers could get free food and water from local people. Beside every marquee or rest station were tannoys blaring out music to encourage and inspire the walkers.

A few miles further along the road, we saw a group of four or five water buffalo grazing on the grass verge. A man riding a bike was unphased by the buffalo as he weaved his way around them and continued onwards. It was at that exact moment that, on the opposite side of the road, the loud speaker outside a marquee was turned on. Suddenly, in an ear – splitting, thunderous din, there was an outburst of music. Frightened and startled, as one, the water buffaloes were put to flight. They charged down the grass verge. The poor, unsuspecting cyclist was overtaken by rampaging buffaloes. Several of them buffeted into the bicycle in their mad frenzy to escape. The cyclist flew through the air; his bicycle flew through the air. Regaining his feet, as if nothing unusual had happened, he dusted down the seat of his trousers, picked up his bike, mounted it, and continued cycling down the verge.

---oOo---

A tour of South Africa in 2012 took us from Cape Town, along the Garden Route, to Durban. From Durban we travelled north for about two and a half hours into Kwazulu - Natal province. Travelling along the N2 road, we bypassed Empangeni and

Richard's Bay until we reached our destination of Lake St. Lucia. The Great St. Lucia Wetlands is a conservation area and includes a substantial marine reserve. Lake St. Lucia is separated from the ocean by a line of dunes, covered in forest vegetation, that tower to 200 metres in height. Arriving at the boat terminal we were transferred onto a fifteen seater, flat bottomed, Safari Boat for a two hour cruise along the lake into the estuary.

As we went we saw Nile crocodiles basking on the sandy banks, pods of hippos wallowing in the water, African Fish Eagles wheeling overhead and many other birds including white breasted and reed cormorants, African jacomas, pied and giant kingfishers, hornbills, egrets, terns, spoonbill, stilts, grey and goliath herons, black winged plovers and many more.

The boat skirted close to the banks, weaving past the hippo pods all walking along the bed of the estuary. Hippos don't actually swim. On the bank hippos were browsing and feeding amongst the reeds. As we were cruising close to the bank, a baby hippo galloped from the sandy shore and splashed into the water just in front of the boat. Alarmed by the baby's actions, the mother charged after it, thrashing into the water. Being the third largest land animal, standing about five feet tall, at 12-15 feet long and weighing in at 2500-3000 pounds, the mother hippo made quite a splash, sending ranks of waves which rocked the boat. Then, sensing that all was well, both mother and baby wallowed in the cooling water. Hippos can run at about 20 m.p.h and the mother certainly entered the water at a rapid rate. As things settled down, the pod of hippos enjoyed resting in the water, some wallowing, and some disappearing beneath the surface. They can stay underwater for up to six minutes.

---oOo---

From St. Lucia we continued onwards through Swaziland to the Limpopo province. Bordering Limpopo and Mozambique is the Kruger National Park. We embarked on a safari in a Kruger safari vehicle. It wasn't long before we spotted rhinos grazing, zebras, herds of buffalo and a pack of hyenas. The hyenas slunk across the road in front of us and gathered together in a small ravine. As we continued deeper into the park we stopped to view the graceful movement of small clusters of giraffes. The guide-driver heard on his walkie-talkie that somewhere further on to the west a lioness and her cub had been spotted. Driving up and down the stretch of road where the sighting had been reported, we finally came to a stop and waited. After a while the lioness was spotted climbing to the top of a small, rocky outcrop. We waited quite a while until she stalked off into the undergrowth but we didn't catch sight of her cub.

It was on the way back from the lioness sighting that we stopped to view a small herd of elephants browsing amongst the trees, just off the road. Suddenly, from behind a cluster of trees, a huge, lumbering bull elephant appeared. He was much bigger than all the other elephants and his large ears flapped vigorously in what appeared to be annoyance and agitation. Reaching up with his trunk, he gathered a bunch of leaves from a tree and gobbled them up. Then, as if in annoyance that this was not sufficient, he backed off, bowed his head, and then lunged forward with his huge tusks. Pushing and bucking his head several times, he uprooted the whole tree and threw it to the ground. Then, in triumphant satisfaction, he grazed contentedly on the leaves of the fallen tree.

Back home, in 2014, an item on the news caught our attention. In Kruger National Park, on 30th. December, 2013, a couple in a blue car had a lucky escape when a large, rogue bull elephant attacked and flipped over the car several times. One of the passengers was a British teacher who was admitted to hospital having been gored in the thigh by one of the elephant's tusks. A South African man accompanying her was reported to have suffered less serious injuries.

Although there are quite a few elephants in the Kruger Park, this elephant's demeanour and behaviour was very much like the tree toppling bull which we had encountered in 2012.

---oOo---

Our South African tour came to an end as we reached Johannesburg. The following morning we were to fly from Jo'burg up to Livingstone in Zambia for our visit to Victoria Falls.

The Royal Livingstone Hotel was a beautiful hotel made up of rooms in small housing units. From the balcony of our room we looked out upon the sweeping lawns which stretched down to the very banks of the Zambesi. It was only a ten minute stroll along the banks of the Zambesi to Victoria Falls.

Once settled in we followed the river and arrived at the first viewpoint of the Falls. Even though water levels were lower because it was their summer,

Victoria Falls were very impressive. We visited all three viewing points until we came to the dead end where you overlooked the gorge with the river running on. Opposite, the Zambesi flowed under the high Victoria Falls Bridge which leads into Zimbabwe. As we looked out we saw people bungee jumping from the bridge. This was the same spot where, in the previous year, a young Australian lady had bungee jumped and the cord snapped. She fell headlong into the river 364 feet below with her feet still tied. She was being swept towards the rapids. She managed to avoid any crocodiles and was able to swim ashore to safety. Luckily she had only suffered a fractured collar bone and severe bruising.

On our way back through the grounds of the Royal Livingstone to our hotel room, we suddenly saw a zebra grazing nonchalantly. Then, further on, we were stunned as we rounded the corner, skirting the tree lined edge of the path, to come face to face with a giraffe. We stopped. The giraffe was no more than ten feet away from us. Blinking its great, dark eyes, it glanced at us, and then nonchalantly carried on feeding on the juicy leaves at the top of the tree next to us.

11. Human Antics

Driving in South Island, New Zealand, we had reached Kaikoura on the east coast, north of Christchurch. We stayed in a motel for a few days. Whilst we were there we went on a whale and dolphin watching boat from the aptly named Whaleway Station, Whaleway Road. Sperm whales spouted less than 100 metres off our bows. Breaking the surface, they would dive, their huge flukes protruding vertically above the surface before they disappeared underwater. Dusky dolphins leapt and played and flashed beneath the boat.

From Kaikoura we travelled south to Christchurch. We stayed a while in this beautiful city, visiting the cathedral and the International Antarctic Centre. We also went on a punt down the River Avon. The young man with the pole propelled us along the river through the beautiful parkland. We asked him if this was a permanent job. He replied that he was on a gap break – in an American Accent. He said that the criteria for the job was being able to stand upright on the back of the punt and being able to wield the long pole. So any thoughts we had of a local New Zealand student supplementing his income was immediately eradicated.

Continuing on from Christchurch we were heading for Mount Cook. En route we stopped at the Church of The Good Shepherd. Behind the small altar the window was not stained glass but just plain glass. Looking out onto the powder blue Lake Tekapo and the dark mountains, we realized why there was no need for stained glass. The church was built in 1935. Close to the church is the well-known bronze statue of a New Zealand collie sheepdog. It was modelled on a local dog called Haig. It was commissioned by Mackenzie Country residents in recognition of the important role of the sheepdog in their livelihoods.

From here our journey led us to Mount Cook. On arrival at the Hermitage Hotel we were told that we were lucky to see the snowcapped peak of Aoraki Mount Cook against an unblemished blue sky. The receptionist said that this was the first day the peak had been visible during the last month or so and, that more often than not it was hidden in cloud. It was said that it was only clearly visible about a dozen times during the year. Mount Cook was 12,349 feet (3764 metres) high but since 2014 is listed as 12,218 feet (3724 metres) due to rock slide and subsequent erosion. It is the highest mountain in New Zealand and helped Sir Edmund Hillary to develop his climbing skills in preparation for the conquest of Everest.

Our travels continued from here southwards to Queenstown. We stayed in Queenstown for three to four days enjoying the many sights and activities including a jet boat ride along the River Dart, a boat trip up Doubtful Sound and walks along the shore of Lake Wakatipu. Walking along the River Dart we saw the marqueed village for the location filming of the Narnia Chronicles, *Prince Caspian* and the backdrop of the *Misty Mountains* in *The Lord of The Rings* film.

From Queenstown we drove up the west coast towards the Fox Glacier and our final destination of the Franz Joseph Glacier.

This was one of our longest driving stretches. Eventually we arrived at the Rainforest Retreat, our accommodation in Franz Joseph village. Weary and tired, we parked the car and went over to the reception lodge. Inside, behind the bar-like desk, stood two, well-built New Zealand ladies.

'Have you had a good journey?' asked one of the ladies.

'Yes, we've come from Queenstown,' I replied, 'so I'm a bit stiff.'

Almost immediately they both said in unison, 'Which one of us brought that on?'

Realising what they meant, I laughed and said, 'Probably both of you.'

---oOo---

The antics of people in other countries, especially on the roads, can vary from unusual to eccentric to downright dangerous. Our travels by coach in India illustrated this very thing – in the downright dangerous category!

Journeying from Agra to Jaipur, we ran into heavy traffic on a dual carriageway. Needless to say, there were no lane markings and no lane discipline. At least four lines of traffic sprawled across what was really a two lane carriageway. Traffic weaved in and out, moving across the lines at will, regardless of how close they cut in front of other vehicles. There was much use of breaks but no hysterical Italian style horn sounding. In fact all users treated this as the normality and were utterly calm and sanguine about it. Our carriageway at least was moving at a steady speed. Looking across to the other side of the dual carriageway, we could see that the traffic was at a standstill. The traffic jam went on for miles. But even so I never thought that the lack of crash barriers between the carriageways was a problem. But then, we were driving in India!

Moving steadily on, everything seemed to be as normal as possible; our coach pulling out and missing backs of cars by fractions; other vehicles pulling in front of us; brakes squealing; but no one sounding their horns in annoyance. Everyone on the road knew the one rule – that there were no rules! But, suddenly, a lorry driver on the opposite carriageway had become impatient, and decided to cross over to our carriageway where the traffic was still moving. He proceeded to weave his way through the oncoming traffic. Except for all the passengers on our coach, no one seemed perturbed; no one seemed surprised; no one sounded their horn; no one shook fists or uttered foul language; everyone accepted it as normal. Others were spurred on by this initiative. First, a boy on a bicycle came towards us, then a car, then another. Nobody crashed; nobody was hurt.

We encountered a different road transport experience when we arrived at Jaipur, known as the *Pink City* because of the colour of the stone from which the buildings were made. It was founded in 1727 and among its attractions is the Amber Palace. We left our hotel at 8.30 a.m. to go on a rickshaw ride. Arriving at the square we were assigned to a rickshaw driver. Our driver was a thin, small man who must have been about seventy years old. Off we went in a procession up the main street, stopping at the Hawa Mahal (Palace of The Winds). This had been built in 1799 by the poet Sawai Pratap Singh for the ladies of the royal household to observe street festivals unseen from the outside. Traffic through the streets was heavy and our driver had to pedal hard and negotiate cars, bicycles, buses and lorries. We were approaching a roundabout where traffic from all directions seemed to converge. The word chaos does not do justice to what lay ahead of us. Our driver now had to pedal uphill towards the roundabout. He had enlisted the help of a younger man to help him by pushing us up the hill. Once at the top he paid him with a coin and we continued on. Rickshaws dodged car fenders almost touching them. Cars honed in from every direction only inches from our rickshaw. Just ahead of us, creeping onto the roundabout, one of our rickshaw party cut in front of a motor cyclist causing him to veer left suddenly. The motor cyclist was duly annoyed and, in what must have been Indian swear words, edged alongside the rickshaw driver, shouted at him and clouted him across the back of the head. The rickshaw driver just froze and obviously, in his position in the order of status could not and did not retaliate or say anything. However, his two English passengers gave the motor cyclist a good telling off. He merely looked at them with incredulity and moved off. As we approached the end of the ride our driver turned to us and said, 'Big tip, very heavy.' (Must go on a diet!) Although we were advised that the tour guide would tip them all we felt sorry for him and duly gave him a tip.

---oOo---

29 kilometres from Oudtshoorn, South Africa, just before the world famous Garden Route, at the head of the picturesque Cango valley, lie the spectacular underground system of the Klein Karoo – the Cango Caves. They are situated in a limestone ridge parallel to the Swartberg Mountains. On our way to the start of the Garden Route, we stopped off to visit these

Cango Caves. As we entered the caves, we were greeted by an instant rush of warm air and humidity. In the past, the Bushmen lived in the topmost system of caves, believing their ancestors inhabited the caves below. In the entrance we were directed to diagrams on the wall. These indicated the height and width of tunnels and potholes in relation to etchings of human bodies. This was the Adventure Route and was a network of narrow and very narrow tunnels and chambers. The mural also showed the Standard Route, which was a system of large caves, passageways and chambers. Warnings about size, weight, fitness and health convinced us to choose the Standard Route. We enjoyed a wonderland of dripstone clusters bathed in vermilion and gold. The main feature within the huge Van Zyl's Hall is Cleopatra's Needle said to be over 150,000 years old.

It measures nine metres in height. Other formations are the Madonna and Child, the Leaning Tower of Pisa and the Pulpit of the Cathedral. Inside Lot's Chamber are the biblical Lot and his family carved in stalagmites.

How wise we were to stick to the Standard Route. At the entrance there were warnings stating that if you are pregnant, suffer from claustrophobia, high blood pressure, asthma or any muscular ailments, then this tour is not suitable. It looked like a venture for trained and experienced potholers! As we toured the Standard Route, the guide told us about the Adventure Route and its recent problems.

You enter the Adventure Route by Jacob's Ladder with over 200 steps leading through the Grand Hall and then the low confines of Lumbago Alley. Lumbago Alley is 85 metres long and, for the most part the roof is low, seldom exceedingly 1.2 metres. Steps lead down into cellar like chambers called King Solomon's Mines. An iron ladder ascends from King Solomon's Mines into the Devil's Chimney Section. First you crawl through the Tunnel of Love, a low passage some 74 cms high, narrowing at one point to 30cm. This brings you to the Ice Chamber and then into The Coffin, a hexagonal shaped hole. Before reaching the Devil's Kitchen, with its narrow, steep shaft of about 45 cm wide, you encounter the Post Box. A narrow pothole leads into this cramped rock room which is a dead end so you have to return via the same pothole into the main passage.

The guide told us about two recent incidents in this cave system. Despite warnings at the entrance, there were some human errors of judgment. One pregnant lady (4 – 5 months) arrogantly insisted that she should go on this Adventure Route. Approaching the Post Box she got stuck at its entrance trapping all the others who had entered it. They were trapped for eleven hours before being rescued.

In another incident a well built, bodybuilding rugby player, against all advice, insisted on doing this challenge safe in his own knowledge that he had the strength to pull himself through any narrow passage. Once again he became stuck and struggled to move. On his stomach he forced himself on his elbows along the narrow passage. In doing so he broke several ribs, was in great pain, and could not move. Once again others were trapped as well. It took eight hours to rescue this party!

Human antics on such travels can result in problems or difficult and dangerous situations.

---oOo---

On our South African tour we left the natural wonders of St. Lucia in Kwazula –Natal province where we had encountered hippos wallowing in the water and continued north westwards to a hotel in Ghost Mountain at Mkuze. From here we set off on a scenic mountain drive up to the Ubombo Mountains to visit a typical Zulu homestead. In an open topped jeep we wound our way up a very bumpy, dusty road, passing small communities until we reached the homestead.

The "tour" was conducted by Justice, the eldest son of the family. He had a girl friend who lived 60 km away whom he saw infrequently. However, she had their six and a half year old child. He was saving up his cows in order to provide the dowry for his "bride". He explained the different cultures and traditions of the Zulus. It is very much an extended family culture where the children and grandchildren look up to and look after their elders. The "granny" was walking and working round the homestead. It is suspected that she was over one hundred years old although there were no official documents in the olden days. The daughters of the family move away and go to live with their in laws and the sons build a new house for their families on the compound and so the number of buildings grows.

There is a building that is the kitchen and a building dedicated to their ancestors. It is called the Spirit House where they believe their ancestors abide. It is in here that they announce the news of the family and ask the advice of their ancestors. They bury their dead at the rear of the property. Chickens, goats and dogs are kept and they all roam free. There were several children wandering about, some barefoot. There was some evidence of an electricity supply, but no running water.

---oOo---

Having left the beautiful Garden Route and Kwazula –Natal province in South Africa, we drove into Swaziland. It was raining heavily and had been for two days. We drove to the border and had to be stamped on leaving South Africa. Then we drove on to the border control and had to be stamped to enter Swaziland. The two border posts were so different. The South African border post was well organized in well-kept buildings. The Swaziland border post was a lot more chaotic and was housed in "sheds" that were leaking with torrents of muddy water everywhere. In

Swaziland there is a major problem with aids and there were boxes of free condoms on display.

Once in Swaziland the spectacular scenery was bathed in mist and rainfall. We stopped for petrol and were passed by a young man who was naked apart from a sweatshirt. Presumably he would have been completely naked but for the heavy rain.

We arrived at our hotel – The Royal Swazi Spa. This was apparently the best hotel in Swaziland. It is situated in the Ezulwini valley on the old Mbabane road. Mbabane is the capital of Swaziland. It boasted a top - class 18 hole golf course, a casino and spa facilities. The rooms were large and beautifully decorated with a spacious balcony overlooking an outdoor swimming pool. Having settled into our rooms, we went, with our other travelling companion, Anne – Marie O'Sullivan (a nurse from Limerick) to book a table for dinner. We had been told that Swaziland was a polygamous country. Once at the desk I said, 'Could we please book a table this evening for the three of us?'

The gentleman at the desk looked at us with a twinkle in his eyes, turned to his entourage of colleagues, smiled knowingly and said in a loud voice, 'Congratulations!' Then he "high - fived" the nearest of his associates.

'No, - er, no,' I protested. 'This is my wife and this lady is our travelling companion.'

He merely smiled and shook his head as if to show his appreciation for my hold over these two ladies.

12. Sunsets

There are many sunsets to be enjoyed all over the world. These are just some of the ones that we witnessed. The future, hopefully, holds more wonderful sunsets in the many other beautiful locations throughout the world that we have not yet visited. Such elevated wonders which we never truly expect really do make a fulfilling holiday, even down to the less dignified experience of *Mike's Underpants*.

Antigua – Shirley Heights

Whilst holidaying in Antigua we went on an organized trip to The Shirley Heights Lookout to witness the sunset.

From Shirley Heights in Antigua there were wonderful views of English Harbour, Nelson's Dockyard and the Caribbean Sea. In the distance we could see the islands of Guadalupe and Montserrat. The Lookout is 490 feet (150 m) above sea level. It was a signal station which used flags by day and guns by night to send messages to the capital St. Johns via Great Fort George on Monk's Hill. It was a military complex which included guard house, magazine, kitchen, officer's quarters, parade grounds, a 40 bed hospital, canteen and cemetery.

Awaiting the start of sunset, we listened to the steel band and sipped drinks with the smoky odour of a barbecue in our nostrils. We stood and looked out as the sun began dipping below the horizon. As the sun's rays lit up the sky it was then that another phenomenon occurred which was to grab everybody's attention.

To the south and west of Shirley Heights was the darkening outline of the island of Montserrat. As the sun was setting behind the island we saw a billowing plume of smoke rapidly ascend into the sky. It was 18th. July, 1995 and the previously dormant Soufriere Hills volcano was erupting. The darkening sky was lit by the setting sun and against this moved the ominous tower of smoke.

The southern part of the island was evacuated. As a British Overseas Territory, in recognition of this disaster, in 1998 the people of Montserrat were granted full residency rights in the United Kingdom, allowing them to migrate if they chose. British citizenship was granted in 2002.

The deepening blue of the sky was fringed with orange, yellow and red as the blood red sun sank, tingeing English Harbour and the Caribbean with an eerie pink-orange wash. Headlands and islands were black silhouettes.

Bali – Tannah Lot

Tannah Lot is a Hindu temple located at Beraban village in the Kediri district on the south coast of Bali, 25 kilometres from Denpaser. It was a Hindu shrine built to worship God in its manifestation as *The God of Sea* (God Baruna), in order to get prosperity. It stands on a rock outcrop in the sea. According to legend it is protected by holy sea snakes. Tannah means "land"; Lot means "the sea". It resembles a small island floating on the sea.

From our hotel in Nusa Dua we had travelled to Tannah Lot to witness the world famous sunset. Sitting on the hillside opposite the temple, we waited in anticipation of the sun disappearing below the distant horizon of the ocean.

The glowing orb of the sun seemed to grow in intensity and size as it sank to the horizon. Sky and sea became inflamed, a golden cloak which produced a stunning background to the black form of rock and temple now etched in silhouette.

Cambodia – Angkor Wat

Another world famous sunset occurs at Angkor Wat temple. After a tour of Vietnam we travelled into Cambodia to stay in Siem Reap. From here we went to visit the magnificent temple complex of Angkor

Wat. We visited the many temples including Angkor Wat temple itself and Angkor Thom temple. But the most exciting, mysterious and stunning was Ta Prohm temple. It is located about one kilometer east of Angkor Thom. It remains in much the same condition as it was discovered. Jungle surrounds the temple with the majestic and spectacular Spung trees (thitpok trees – Tetrameles Nudiflora) and Silk Cotton trees (Ceiba Pentandra) dominating the ruins. It is no surprise that this temple site was used as the location for the film *Lara Croft:Tomb Raider*, starring Angelina Jolie. The huge buttress trunks of these trees frame and protect the tomb entrances and roots coil, tentacle – like, onto the temple walls in a deadly grip. The whole forms a lattice pattern choking the temple walls and looking like runnels of candle wax which have hardened and moulded onto the sandstone structure.

Having visited the temple complex during the morning, we returned late at the end of the afternoon to witness the sunset. We trudged onward uphill to Phnom Bakheng temple. It is a short distance from the Angkor Wat temple and, built at the end of the ninth century, was dedicated to Shiva. This temple is on top of a hill and we had to climb up the steep, narrow steps to get to the ruins. Once on top you have a 360 degree, unobstructed, view over the temple complex and the jungle to the west. Being such a popular place to watch the sunset, it tends to get crowded.

As the sun began to set, the temples on the eastern side were silhouetted against a glowing, orange and red sky. To the west, the sun was a fiery, white ball as it began to sink below the horizon. Palm trees and jungle trees were mounted in a black diorama against a golden sky.

Australia – Uluru

Uluru (Ayres Rock) is a sandstone monolith which dominates the desert-steppe landscape. It lies south west of Alice Springs in the Northern territory of Australia. It is the largest rock monolith in the world.

From our hotel complex, just outside the National Park, we travelled in the late afternoon into the park to view the effects of the setting sun on Uluru. At a view point facing directly onto the red sandstone rock, tables and chairs had been set up. Here we could view the phenomenon as we sipped sparkling wine and enjoyed canapes. As the sun set behind Uluru, the arcing, moody dark blue sky became tinged on the horizon with a delicate yellow-orange fringe. The rock became bright orange in the intensified sun's rays. Then it began its changes of colour. The orange changed to gold as the sun slipped further to the horizon. Then gold became red and then deep red which melded into a puice-like blue and then purple. In the dying light Uluru became a black mass silhouetted against a dark blue sky lit at the horizon by red and golden flares.

Death Valley is another place where the setting sun causes a kaleidoscope of colours on the cliffs, bluffs and desert basin. As mentioned earlier we stayed overnight at Furnace Creek Ranch. That evening the setting sun set the rocky crags ablaze with ever changing colours, until, reaching the horizon, the black silhouettes of crag and gulley stood in eerie silence against the dark blue sky scarred by the red tongues of cloud which fanned out high above the total blackness of the desert.

Peru – The Floating Reed Islands of Lake Titicaca

Having visited Cuzco in order to climatise before visiting Machu Picchu, we travelled on to Puno on the shores of Lake Titicaca. Lake Titicaca straddles the border between Peru and Bolivia in the Andes. It is one of South America's largest lakes and is the world's highest navigable body of water.

Our hotel looked out onto the lake and, in the distance, the Floating Islands of Lake Titicaca. These islands are made and remade from the totora reeds which provide home, livelihood and transport forms for the Uros tribe who live there.

We went on a half hour boat ride from Puno to Santa Maria, one of the largest of the islands. The totora is a cattail type rush which grows naturally in the lake. It has extremely thick and dense roots which are attached to wooden poles driven into the bed of the lake. The Uros pile gathered reeds onto these roots. These are compacted as more layers are stacked on top. The top layer rots and must be replaced regularly. Disembarking from the boat, we walked out onto the island. The surface was uneven and it was spongy to walk on.

The Uros also create houses from the reeds. The roofs are waterproof but don't prevent humidity. The residents showed us around their homes. They wore layers of woolen clothing to protect them against cold, wind and sun. They continue living there by fishing. They sell any surplus catch on the mainland.

Weaving is another occupation and they produce clothing for themselves and embroidered handicrafts to sell to tourists. Many women still wear derby hats and full skirts. They also catch shore birds and ducks for their eggs and food. There were lots of cats roaming the island. These are kept to control rats.

There are tiny outhouse islands which are used as toilets. The ground roots absorb the waste. Inside the reed huts cooking fires are built on layers of stones to protect the reeds. Stepping inside one hut, there was an Uros Indian sat on a reed bed watching a small black and white television which was perched high on the wall. An aerial lead wire was threaded through the roof and attached to a small satellite dish. This was one sign of the Uros Indians adopting modern technology. Moored along the jetties of these islands were their reed boats. There were long, shallow, canoe-like boats for commuting from island to island and for fishing. But we went aboard a large reed boat which had two upturned neck-like bows and two matching ones at the stern. The prows were fashioned into the heads of creatures which looked like dragons, being reminiscent of Viking longships. Oarsmen paddled up to the next island. Disembarking, we found ourselves in front of a watch tower made from reeds. A ladder led up to the platform and, attached to a wooden perch there was a large condor. The Uros were charging a dollar to climb up for a photo opportunity with the condor.

That evening, from the shoreline lawns of the hotel, the setting sun cast bright white ribbon reflections across the dark waters of the lake. And the blackening sky, lined at the horizon in a silvery glow, picked out the black shapes of the Floating Islands.

Egypt – The Nile at Luxor and Karnak Temple

We were staying at a hotel in Luxor. Here, the swimming pool was almost bordering the River Nile. The views across the Nile to the green cultivated fields, edged by palm trees, were indeed, very striking. Beyond this green strip was the desert, the Valley of the Kings and the Theban Hills. Before dining, our first delight of the evening was to climb to one of the upper balcony terraces and view the sunset. The sun dipped below the far horizon of the Theban Hills, turning the sky blood red. The backdrop of blood red sky was over layered by the black silhouettes of palm trees on the opposite bank. The river itself presented a foreground of liquid black striped with the reflection of the red sky.

Not far from our Luxor hotel was the temple at Karnak. The massive pillars of the temple are awe inspiring. At sunset these columns were lit in golden hues. The sun was a great, white, shining ball. As it sank to the horizon it turned the sky dark blue with pale orange fringes. This formed an otherworldly backdrop to the black silhouettes of obelisks, pillars, temple walls and palm trees.

Costa Rica – The Tarcoles River

On our tour of Costa Rica we arrived at Tarcoles. The Tarcoles River flows from the mountains of the Central Valley and drains into the Gulf of Nicoya in the Pacific Ocean.

In the late afternoon we embarked upon a Jungle Crocodile Safari on the Tarcoles River. We saw many crocodiles basking on the mud banks and in amongst the mangroves. At one point we pulled slowly into the bank and stopped next to a huge crocodile which lay motionless just below the surface of the water.

Chugging up and down the river, we spotted many different species of birds. In fact we saw 43 different birds which included: a frigate bird, anhinga, ibis, spoonbill, six different types of heron (Great Blue, Little Blue, Tricolour, Bare Throated, Green and Yellow Crowned), egrets, jacanas, stilts, turkey and black vultures, peregrine falcon, osprey, scarlet macaw, three types of kingfisher (Ringed, Amazon and Green) and many more.

As the afternoon wore on we sailed upriver to its mouth which opened into the Gulf of Nicoya. The estuary was separated from the ocean with a sandbank. The boat remained stationary as we watched the sun set over the Pacific. The large, orange, molten ball of the sun dipped to the horizon. As it began to sink, it lit the sky with orange wisps. The ocean and river rippled with an orange-red glow, turning bluish and then purple as the sun's rays stretched across the water in a shimmering, golden band. And, as we watched in awed silence, a flock of pelicans flew across the golden sky and roosted in the tall jungle trees now becoming silhouettes on the left bank of the estuary. Scores of pelicans roosted in the trees, flying and gliding to and fro across the magical, sunset sky.

The Dolomites and an explosive sunset

There are many sunsets to be enjoyed all over the world. These are just some of the ones we witnessed. The future, hopefully, holds more wonderful sunsets in the many other beautiful locations throughout the world that we have not yet visited.

As an endnote I recall one memorable sunset in the Dolomite Mountains. Having driven down from Innsbruck with Mike and Margaret we took up residence in a beautiful three storied farmhouse perched on a hill overlooking the valley and the distant crags of the Dolomites. The Dolomites are sometimes known as the "Pale Mountains" because they are made of carbonate rock dolomite. There are 18 peaks in the chain which rise to above 3000 meters.

We had accommodation in one of the two upper rooms which both had balconies facing out over the valley to the impressive rocky peaks of the Dolomites. The view was magnificent with vertical walls, sheer cliffs, and deep long valleys. Towering steeples and pinnacles of rock in a huge serrated range stood before us.

One evening I was sitting on the balcony by myself. A solid wooden screen separated our balcony from the one next door. As I sat awaiting the others I could hear the quiet conversation of our neighbors who were speaking in German. Then the sun began to slide behind the mountains which took on a rosy glow thus earning this range the name of Rosengarten. I shouted to the others inside to come and see the sunset. First on the scene was Mike. Unknown to him the German couple on the next balcony were viewing the sunset in reverent silence. Mike marked his entrance with a mind blowing, rip snorting passing of wind.

And in reply to this I said, 'Ah, welcome, Herr Doctor Fahrtenarsen.' This was followed by uncontrollable sniggers from the balcony next door.

Mike mouthed, 'Why didn't you tell me?' and sat down quietly.

Shortly after, our two wives appeared. They had missed the explosive start to the sunset. But, sipping wine, we all sat and watched the changes in colour on the rock faces of the Dolomites – from rosy pink, to deep pink, to deep red.

Such elevated wonders which we never truly expect, really do make a fulfilling holiday and other less dignified events which we never truly expect belong to *Mike's Underpants*.

Epilogue

These Tales of Travel began with the start of my longing to travel, my passion for geography and all the places in the world which fired my imagination. Then I dreamt of visiting the countries and continents which I had learned about in my studies. Since those early days, I have managed to see some of the places which were brought to life in the classroom at Cowley Boys' School, St. Helens by an inspirational Geography teacher – Mr. Rimmer.

But did the reality match up to my imagination?

Where the places as magical as my dreaming, younger self thought?

Did these places and things live up to my expectations?

The answer, as I hope you have realized, is that they did – except, of course, for

Mike's Underpants!

Printed in Poland
by Amazon Fulfillment
Poland Sp. z o.o., Wrocław